INDIGO RISING

by G.W. Hardin

INDIGO RISING

Awakening the Powers of the Children of the New Earth

G.W. Hardin

DreamSpeaker Creations, Inc.
Fort Collins, Colorado • 2005

All of this story is based on actual events. Some names have been changed to protect individuals' privacy. Some scenes have been combined into a single scene for the purpose of bettering the story line.

First printing: January 2005

Publication Data
      Hardin, G.W.
      Indigo Rising:
           Awakening the Powers of the Children of the New Earth
      Family, New Consciousness, Inspiration
           pp. 220

      ISBN 1-893641-07-4
      1. Family 2. New Consciousness 3. Inspiration

Cover design: Ken Elliott and G.W. Hardin
Book design: G.W. Hardin

Set in 12 point Times New Roman typeface
Printed in the United States of America
Lightning Source - LaVergne, TN

DEDICATION

Dedicated to all the Children of the New Earth, who have given me hope I never thought possible in our time.

ACKNOWLEDGMENTS

*T*o those who made this all possible in big and little ways, especially Janet Hardin (who convinced me to bring this book forward), Ken Elliott, Meryl Sloane and Carol Mahoney. I give special thanks to the Elders who have helped create possibilities for the Circle of Indigos in Fort Collins and Boulder: Paul Holden, Lucie Blanchard, Marion Weiss, and Cheryl Rennels. Particular gratitude goes to Mark Leone and Victoria Ponte Leone who made the completion of this project possible. What amazingly wonderful people. May all be blessed with such friends as these.

Contents

INDIGO RISING

INTRODUCTION

*S*ince humanity began, one generation has been at war with the other over cultural change. Since Cain and Abel, human differences have all too often served little purpose other than to issue forth strife. Has humanity ever had a generation that did not have to face war of some kind? Those days are soon to be over. A phenomenon is rising before us where sons no longer follow fathers into coal mines or corporate America. Daughters look at their mothers and question the extremes of taking refuge either in historical values or in herculean theater that urges them to play not only cook, chauffeur, caregiver, and lover, but also protector, leader, and businesswoman. Yes, these Children of the New Earth have been born with eyes that see too much. They do not like what they see. Does that mean the older generation blinds them, or at least puts blinders on them? Believe me, it has been tried. But something greater than war rumbles within their souls. The day will come when they will not be denied; they will not stop at compromise. The rumbling travels through families, school systems, institutions, and now through society itself. No longer can our older generation go whistling through the graveyard. An undeniable force bridges this new generation to the graves of our ancestors and to the hopes of a better future. This bridge over troubled waters is not made of iron and steel but of new awareness and miraculous wonders inherent in the human condition, which somehow were lost or forgotten across time.

A great shift has swept across the Earth with only the few truly noticing. The blessings of the sons will begin the healing of the fathers. The corporate mentality that has kidnapped fatherhood from hearth and home is being replaced by a revolution that cannot be stopped because it cannot be understood in full.

What follows is the story of two generations. Such a story has not been told because such a story was not tellable. As much as the uncertainty of quantum physics has eclipsed Newtonian laws, so has the emerging consciousness of a new generation begun to eclipse the rigid thinking, the in-the-box restrictions, and the limited abilities of its forebears. No prophecy is any longer valid, and no preconceived notions can stem the tide of this collective sea change.

This new generation has been labeled the "Indigos," the "Crystals," or the "Starseed Children," among a growing list of names. But the truth be told, no label will work, for this generation rejects labels. The labeling suits only the older generation that is trying to figure out the younger. And none is served by this attempt to corral. Such differentiation only echoes Solomon's words: it is folly.

Listen to this true story as the mistakes of an older generation no longer haunt the newer. The sins of the fathers are no longer visited upon the sons. The Earth begins to look less and less like a treasure to be dug up or owned, and more and more like a garden to be cared for and harvested. This rising generation of young adepts inherently sees the big picture: the value of spirit over success, healing over warring, and cooperative creation over survival of the fittest. The Internet has secretly replaced "supply and demand," "scarcity of resources," and "planned obsolescence" with exponentially increasing access to information, unlimited thinking, and a service-dominated economy that needs only ideas on which to thrive. Amazingly, these youth also see a treasure in Elders, whom we have labeled "the elderly." These young adepts seek out their wisdom as if it were gold, while our society warehouses the aged as castoffs of a forgotten time or as spent shells of a rifle.

At the heart of what you are about to read lies a love story that threatens conventional beliefs but inspires unheard-of possibilities. For love is the least understood human trait of all. Possibly because it is also the essence of the godly. These Children of the New Earth hold in their hands the best of what it means to be human and the undeniable truth that even quantum physics has discovered: all of life is one. What lies in wait for a world that tries to hang onto separation, judgment of others, terrorism, and domination? More love. We are headed toward a transformation that is only sped up by resistance, that is only made more obvious by sabotage, that will end up bending the knee of a stubborn past out of sheer awe — not fear. For these Children of the New Earth are the harbingers of the Age of Miracles and the thousand years of peace. Watch, listen, hear, as what unfolds on these pages and within your lives grows from the faint chirping of crickets to the heavenly rejoicing of angels. A new world has come forth, and a new generation has emerged to shoulder it.

But let us keep this simple. Let us begin with one child and one generation. Let us witness how the old ways are bending knee to the awareness of Oneness. Let us acknowledge how the new is *not* replacing the old but bridging it to the Oneness. The very concepts of new and old must disappear in a universe of the One. It is quantum magic that is unfolding around us. Let the magic show begin.

Little did Jeed know that he would become a symbol of his generation's preparation for the arrival of what many would call the "Indigos." Much has been written already about what an Indigo is and is not, and much more will continue to be written in an effort to define a phenomenon that escapes definition. Indigos will tell you today that they (or anyone) cannot be put into boxes. Untold wrongs and sufferings have arisen in our world trying to put people and concepts into tight little boxes.

To transcend or to transform, people have to think, feel, and operate outside of the box. Jeed's generation has come to prepare a place for the first generation of the Children of the New Earth by fomenting great change, hoping to create of a new world that cannot be kept in a box.

BOOK ONE

EXPLORING THE POWERS
OF INITIATION

Chapter One

THE CHILD

*f*rom an early age, Jeed began his own rites of initiation, which would prepare him for the boggling path to come. Jeed's parents were the first to try and keep Jeed in his boxy room. Later, they would go to even greater extents to squelch his power. What cannot be forced to change is often isolated or even imprisoned. What animal, when caged or isolated, does not resort to its basic instincts? And if those instincts cannot save the spirit of the animal, then what animal does not go stir-crazy or die?

Jeed's childhood was a dance with the Devil. His memories haunted him for years with feelings of being vulnerable, helpless, and afraid. Afraid of his old man beating the tar out of him, afraid of the other kids pouncing on him because he was the runt at school. Even afraid of June bugs on his bedroom window screen at night.

The Illinois summer nights stifled any attempt at sleep with merciless heat and humidity. Open windows offered the only relief in the early '50s; air conditioning was a luxury at the time. Because it was summertime young Jeed always protested that any time was too early for bedtime. Was it a grand conspiracy by all parents, or just his, to get rid of the kids as soon as possible after sunset? The door to Jeed's room was always closed tightly so he couldn't be heard. For a five-year-old, he had a tendency to be persistent. His room, black as an abandoned cave, echoed the sounds of the night through the open window. Why the June bugs congregated on his window screen every night confounded him. The little beasties terrified him with their fat beetle bodies and their barbed feet plucking the wire weave like a cheap harp, as if crying out, "Let me in, let me in." Crazily, they lumbered on some pointless journey, pointless except to haunt him until sleep mercifully carried him away from all the fear.

During daylight, June bugs look rather beautiful with their iridescent reddish-brown bodies, shaped like split acorns. On the weekends, Jeed hunted and imprisoned the beasties in a jar. One by one, he would tie a piece of thread on one of their legs, and hold one end of the thread while forcing the hapless June bug to fly in circles until exhaustion, or until the shackled leg broke off. The aerial show proved to be a hit with other kids. But during the night, the beetle army gathered on Jeed's window screen, trying to break in and swarm over him in revenge. Clicking, pinging, and popping echoed through his room as they continued their onslaught.

"Mom?" Silence. "Can I have a glass of water?" he would scream at the top of his lungs so as to be heard through the sealed door, down the hallway, and into the living room. Calling for Dad was futile. Shadows of giant June bugs crawled across Jeed's wall next to his bed. "Mom?"

"You had water before you went to bed," Mom screamed back after a mumbling pause, which really was "Oh no, not this again." Several June bugs buzzed with their wings, trying to fly, trying to disconnect their little barbed feet from the wire mesh. Several took flight in small circles, crashing against the screen in battering-ram fashion. Jeed panicked at the thought that they were about to come through the screen. Their monstrous shadows now dove at him on the wall, forcing Jeed to cover himself with his bed sheet.

He hid as long as the heat would allow, and then he screamed, "I have to go to the bathroom!" Was no one going to save him?

"You don't have to go to the bathroom. You went before going to bed." The irritation in Mom's voice was the warning sign that Dad, the Punisher, was about to join the June bugs in their war against Jeed's childhood.

"Now I have to go number two." How was he going to squeeze out any proof of this? He knew the consequences if he didn't. He was beginning to feel trapped.

The bedroom door exploded open, drenching the cavelike room in a flood of light. The June bugs flushed, filling the room with their buzzing. "By God," Dad yelled, "if you don't have to go to the bathroom, you're going to get an ass-beating!" Suspending his son in midair by his left arm, the Punisher whisked Jeed out of the torture chamber with the buzzing applause of the June bugs fading behind him. At least he had escaped the beasties.

"How long are you going to sit there and grunt?" Dad was drunk.

"It doesn't want to come out, Daddy," Jeed whined, hoping for mercy.

"Well, you let me know when it does. I'm going back into the living room." Finally, the desired objective had been met. It usually took another trip to the refrigerator before Jeed would be thought of again. Jeed prayed hopefully, *Please, God, make the beer last a long time.* Yes, Jeed was persistent. But there usually was a price to be paid.

"Are you still there?" Several minutes had passed. "Get off there and get back to bed." This night, there would be no ass-beating. After Jeed climbed back into bed, there came the "Now shut up and go to sleep." The door slammed shut and the platoons of June bugs once more began their onslaught to break through the window screen. Their nasty little barbed feet plucked at the wire again and again.

Oh how I wish I was grown up so I wouldn't be afraid anymore. That was Jeed's nightly prayer. As the shadows dive-bombed at Jeed's head once more and the buzz of many wings echoed with intensity, the terror mounted again. "Mom, I really am thirsty," he yelled even louder.

Silence. Only silence against the attack of June bugs.

Being an Air Force brat, friendship did not come easily to Jeed. Moving from base to base made him feel like the offshoot of a gypsy band, made only worse by his father's long absence from home when moonlighting. His was a life of varying shades of loneliness.

"Hey, Jeed, you wanna join a gang?" Gene made it sound as if he were asking, "Hey, you wanna go buy a popsicle?" Gene was Jeed's best buddy. Although only a year older than Jeed, Gene's twelve-year-old street smarts were easily ten years beyond Jeed's. What Jeed liked most about Gene was his ability to create the most incredible biplanes out of popsicle sticks — sanded to perfection, glued toothpick struts supporting aerodynamic popsicle wings, and actual working popsicle-stick propellers and wheels. The two boys roamed the streets of Travis Air Force Base almost daily picking up discarded popsicle sticks as their summer pastime. But for some reason, this summer had changed Gene.

"What's a gang?" Jeed asked naively. He had heard the word at school, whispered by certain sixth-grade girls, with whom guys like Jeed weren't supposed to associate. These mysterious girls talked to older guys who wore grease in their hair to buttress ducktail haircuts. The Elvis look-alikes wore their jeans down around their hips and flashed switchblade knives to make the girls-you-don't-associate-with gasp. Jeed forever wondered what magic these "greasers" used to keep their jeans from falling to their knees. It wasn't so much that Jeed hated these greasers, he just hated the fact that they looked like Elvis. Elvis made Jeed puke.

"You don't know what a gang is?" Gene was spying out of a square peephole from their secret clubhouse, made of two discarded refrigerator boxes. The blast of the California noonday sun illuminated the sparse interior. It's where they kept their stash of accumulated popsicle sticks.

"No. Do you?"

"Well, yeah."

"Then 'fess up since you know it all." Gene was smart, almost as smart as Jeed, even though Jeed only got ten cents for every A on his report card while Gene got a dollar.

Gene closed up the square hole, casting the two into temporary blindness. This was their favorite place in the whole world to hang out when they weren't making popsicle airplanes. But, now, the heat of the noonday sun was starting to turn the clubhouse more into an oven than a haven. Nighttime worked much better for spying and making secret plans, especially when the two slept together in threadbare blankets under rainless skies.

"Gangs are like clubs, except you beat up people," Gene confessed.

"Doesn't sound like fun to me." At an early age, Jeed was already into nonviolence.

"The other guys say all you have to do is find a chain or pipe or carry a switchblade, and you can cruise the neighborhoods with them looking for someone to rumble with. But to be in the gang, you have to beat up one of the gang members first."

"Golly, Gene, I don't think I could beat up anybody."

"We could go together. Two of us together should be able to beat somebody up." Every bully around loved to pick on Jeed. His shortness still made him the runt of the school, and he would remain so for three more years. But Gene could always be counted on. He was the only person who wouldn't beat Jeed up. It was bad enough getting constant beatings at home, but getting roughed up on a regular basis at school was not only painful, it was humiliating. The thought of beating someone else therefore up intrigued him. So, there the two boys sat in their ovenlike cardboard clubhouse wondering who they would have to beat up so they could be in a gang.

Later, that afternoon, Gene and Jeed searched for discarded chains or pipes instead of popsicle sticks. They never found anything of real weapons-grade quality — and probably just as well. The buddy of Gene's, who had extended the invitation to join the gang, ended up in the hospital that night. Lost a tooth and wore a shiner for a couple of weeks, which the other guys in the gang wowed over.

Gene and Jeed never did talk about joining a gang after that. The two returned to the treasure hunting of high-quality popsicle sticks.

As the summer meandered on, Jeed noticed that Gene's dad was never around. Gene's mom made Kool-Aid for the two but told them it had to be drunk outdoors. She never allowed them to stay in for more than a few minutes (usually to use the bathroom), and that was it. Like some recluse, she kept the drapes closed all the time. Said it was to keep the military housing they lived in cool. But Jeed felt like the place was haunted — except there were no spider webs. The place resembled a hospital in that all the furniture was covered in plastic. Even the carpeting had plastic runners. Why she kept the place so pristine was beyond Jeed. No one ever visited. But Jeed's house wasn't any better. His mom was either drunk or away at the NCO Club getting drunk. If Jeed were ever within shouting distance, he'd be asked to clean up this or that, or get this or that while Mom lounged on the couch watching the new TV. She loved giving orders. Dad was never around. When he wasn't working at the air traffic control tower, he was working at the Buckhorn Tavern in town. Said he had to provide for the family. But Jeed never saw the money go for much of anything other than his mother's hairdos or her booze, although, they usually drove the latest Buick in the neighborhood. When his dad was around, Mom wanted him to take her to the NCO Club. Or she wanted him to beat Jeed for not carrying out her orders that day. He stayed away by choice.

For a long time, Jeed thought about Gene's description of a gang. If he could have just beaten up someone else, he might have joined, might have avoided ever being beaten up again. Jeed was tired of being on the receiving end of beatings. The thought of having comrades who helped you rumble with others sounded intoxicating in a way. With no fathers at home, both Gene and Jeed looked for strength, leadership, safety, and the role of manhood elsewhere. The two had learned nothing from their fathers except escape. The grown-ups called it other names like "work demands," or "providing," or "being too busy." But it was nothing but escape.

An eleven-year-old boy will only watch from the river bank so long. None of Jeed's cousins or distant relatives at the family reunion would play with him. They were all having too much fun playing water tag over by the old wooden bridge that led into the Ohanapecosh Park picnic grounds. How Jeed longed to be able to be like the rest of his kin, to be able to jump from the bridge into the river, trying to escape from being tagged "it." But the water flowed too deeply. Neither of Jeed's parents had taught him how to swim. Whether it was a bathtub, a swimming pool, or a river, Jeed loved the feel of water. Like so many other instances, no one in his young world had taken time to teach him how to enjoy this part of life.

Jeed scanned the reunion for anyone who might serve as welcome company. All of the adults had huddled over by the picnic tables, enjoying their beer, catching up on, if not making up, the latest gossip. As usual, Jeed's mom sat absorbed with her two sisters, the three of them clucking like barnyard hens. Instead of chicken feed, beer fed their appetite for cackling about this and that while they slowly put together the fixings for their famous potato salad.

Jeed's gaze returned to the river. Its beauty, its calm, its coolness beckoned him. The river seemed like his only friend. Taking a confident breath, he waded into his only recourse against boredom. The soothing brown water caressed his ankles. After a while, the river tickled at his knees, and then his thighs. The real test would be dipping his crotch below the waterline. He gasped from the chill as he tested himself. After a few more fanny dips, pride welled up within him at daring to go deeper than he ever had before. As he paralleled the shore, now waist deep, he looked around for approval. None of the adults as much as yawned in his direction, and the other kids by the bridge still found him invisible. The ultimate test would be to wade up to his armpits. Dare he? Staring at the muddy current, dread began to fill him. Perhaps he should go back to shore. But as he turned his back to the river, he found himself taking steps backward instead of forward. Each step exhilarated him, the thrill shooting adrenaline through his now-shivering body. Who needed playmates when worlds were being conquered? What could compare to this daring, this excitement, this challenge?

The next step proved to be his last. With the grace of a falling leaf, Jeed slipped beneath the surface of the river and into a drop-off. Oddly, he felt no fear, no panic, no memory of anything except the exquisite beauty of every single drop of water exploding above his head as his arms mindlessly tried to claw to the surface. With near-reverence, the splendid patterns of bubbles and splash etched his memory permanently, painting themselves against a receding blue sky as his body drifted downward through what seemed like a black tunnel. So quiet, all was so peacefully quiet as he fell into growing blackness and drowned.

No one knew how long his body had hugged the bend of the drop-off. One of the relatives commented to Jeed's aunt about how much fun Jeed seemed to be having, frolicking about by himself in the middle of the river. "But he can't swim," his mom blurted out, overhearing the comment. As she scanned the surface of the river, , noticing only calm, flowing, brown water, her breath quickened. "Where did you last see him?" she demanded. As the relative pointed, both Mom and Aunt Polly plunged into the river, clothes and all. After several dives, they finally found the body and dragged it ashore. Jeed was dead. Of course they tried artificial respiration, as unsophisticated as it was in those days, but Jeed's soul had gone elsewhere.

A brilliant light had replaced the darkness, drenching Jeed in unfathomable love. Never had he known love like this — vibrant, uplifting, ecstatic. From the light a voice spoke. "You have to return, for there is work you are to do."

"But why?" Jeed tried to argue. Before the voice would respond, he felt himself being sucked back into the blackness. Confusion swept around him as he heard the sound of weeping, loud weeping, and many voices. *How can anyone be weeping?* he asked himself. *There is so much love. So much everywhere. Why this sadness? Who is crying?* The wailing and sobbing grew, replacing the expanse of love with increasing confusion. As Jeed searched for the fleeting love, he realized he could feel the love only in one remaining place — his left hand. Why was there only love around his left hand? He opened his eyes to darkness. Where had the sun gone? Then he realized that his body had been covered by an army blanket, recognizing the musty smell from his nights of sleeping in the cardboard clubhouse. Then, a terrible hubbub ensued; orders erupted, asking everyone to clear the way for the park ranger. Once again, Jeed could feel the love around his left hand. He turned his head to find the source, and as he did the shroud of blanket fell away from his face. A small dachshund had crawled under the blanket and was licking his left hand. The owner was just about to retrieve the critter when she let out a bloodcurdling scream.

All heads turned to see that the dead had returned. The din of weeping quickly shrank into silence. Jeed's mom finally managed an "Oh my God! Oh my God!" as she wrapped her arms around him. For the life of him, he could not understand what she was crying about. Why was there so much sadness in this world? And why had the God-Light sent him back?

No one spoke on the trip back home to the air base. Some days later, Jeed decided to ride his bike down to the base swimming pool. He would sit by the pool and watch people swim for hours . For three days, he returned to the pool to continue his vigil. Then, without notice, he jumped into the pool and swam across to the other side. Just like that, he had taught himself to swim. No one had paid any attention. He was just another kid in a crowd of kids. But from that day forward, Jeed knew he was not just any kid. He wasn't sure how he knew, but he knew.

Chapter Two

THE CURSE

*W*hat had the beatific God-Light meant that there was work to do? Over the next thirty-five years Jeed constantly wondered why he had been sent back, not telling a single soul what really had happened. How could he explain what he, himself, didn't understand? Before his mother died, he tried once to tell her the whole story of his the drowning. Inexplicably, she tried to shut him up, almost denying the drowning had ever taken place. He wanted badly to tell her about the God-Light, for he suspected she hadn't many years left, with the condition of her liver and the worsening emphysema caused by her heavy smoking. He wanted her to know what was awaiting her on the other side, but she would have no part of it.

Not long after Jeed married, he received a news from his dad his his mother had passed during the night. The funeral would be held a few days hence. Would he like to be a pallbearer? Jeed despised funerals but agreed to be part of the ceremony, the liturgy. He had expected to hear such news for years. His mother's life had become for him ongoing scenes from an Italian opera, her addictions to nicotine and alcohol poisoning more than her own life.

Throughout the entire funeral, he could not help but feel the very same eyes that had witnessed his drowning so many years ago. He had become a pariah since then, and everyone knew it. No longer would he participate in family gatherings where people became secondary to beer or gossip. No longer could he watch people's spirits slowly die while their bodies awaited the same fate.

Jeed thought the burying of his mother would symbolically also bury the tensions of her long history of questioning his normalcy. His marriage had quelled some of her trying to run his life, but his own confrontation with who he was as a man began to take on torturous implications. Her death seemed to leave no excuses for making her the problem any longer. Strange dreams began to invade his world of playing normal. Even events at work began to pull back the mask of his everyman disguise. How strange the ways of the Divine. Who would know that a simple apple would provoke his complete undoing?

"Here. Catch these beauties," Doug yelled down as he tossed the Gravensteins into Jeed's clutched T-shirt. Winter had lingered late that year while summer had arrived early, making for poor conditions for the highly valued apple. Because of the scarcity of Gravensteins, few of the orchards in Oregon allowed u-pick harvesting, sending most of the crop to warehousers and fruit companies. Doug happened to have an old Gravenstein tree, which reached as high as his three-story house on his back acreage. Dropping the apples from about two stories, Doug said, "That's about it. The rest are out of reach. I'm coming down."

Back on the ground, Jeed and Doug divided their golden treasure. Both men prized themselves for their exceptional canning of homemade applesauce, good enough to win ribbons at the county fair. "We need more," Jeed muttered, wiping the sweat from his eyes.

Even for midsummer, this was an unusually hot day. "I'll climb all the way to the top. Gotta pole I can use?" Doug handed an old hoe to his friend as Jeed started the climb up the old tree. As he reached the top branches, bark dust from dead lichens and dried moss showered over him, peppering his yellow T-shirt with powdery specks. Using his left hand to anchor himself to flimsy limbs and the other to shake the hoe, the last of the Gravensteins fell into Doug's waiting hands below. As Jeed stared down at the two baskets of apples, he thought *Ahhh. Enough apples for two batches of canning. First a nap, then canning.* He was exhausted. The two friends laughed heartily as Jeed nearly fell to the ground climbing out of the tree. Their applesauce would be the envy of the town.

For Jeed, the drive home felt good as the breeze dried most of his sweat-soaked T-shirt. Not bothering to unload the booty from the trunk, he headed into the house. The only thing he wanted to see was his pillow. Sleep quickly took him after he fell face first into the disheveled bed. His wife would be pleased with the aroma of cooked apples after working the weekend shift at the hospital.

As he awoke, Jeed discovered a burning itch covering his chest. *Guess I'd better jump into the shower and get rid of the grime*, he thought. As he peeled his clothes off, he noticed the peppery residue on the sheets and pillow. *Better change the bed after the shower*, he concluded. Nattie was a patient woman, but not that patient. After leaving the hot shower, Jeed peered at his bony body in the mirror. The itching had subsided some but red dots had begun to cover his shoulders and chest. Chalking the rash up to the hot shower, Jeed threw on a clean T-shirt and jeans and headed to the kitchen. Applesauce called.

The next morning, Jeed woke to the worst itching he'd ever felt. Another visit to the mirror revealed that the redness had spread. Noticing how small blisters had raised along his sternum, Jeed groaned with the thought of having to endure poison oak. A quick trip to the doctor yielded the usual prescriptions, along with a syringe full of hydrocortisone in his rump. The physician commented, however, that the skin condition didn't really show the same symptoms as poison oak. How right he would be. After the steroids wore off, the whole itching and reddening process began all over again. This time Jeed let it take its course.

In a matter of a few days, his entire chest area resembled a radiation burn. Hundreds of tiny blisters burst, weeping an orange ooze. New blisters appeared in other areas of his torso, spreading the redness. The mirror now reflected what looked like a scene from *Star Trek*, as if his chest having been blasted by a Klingon phaser. Clothing was out of the question. Drying ooze glued his undershirt to his body. The only way to remove the shirt was to soak himself in a hot shower until the shirt would release. Scabs began to form as well. Work at Hewlett-Packard would have to be missed.

Sleep became impossible as the itchiness turned incessant. The only comfort came from turning the shower on to near-scalding hot and drenching the afflicted areas. The heat from the water jets turned his entire upper body into a mass of pin pricks, confusing the skin with mixed sensations of agony and ecstasy. After a few minutes, a strange pleasure would sweep across his torso, almost to the point of orgasm, his stomach muscles convulsing from the overload of sensation, dropping him to his knees. The ritual would end with a deep-throated moan as he crawled out of the shower stall on all fours. By this time, Nattie would be awake, asking the same question, "Can I help in any way?" and she would get the same answer. There was nothing that could be done.

One night, the sleep deprivation took its toll. Hallucinations haunted Jeed. Fire beings entered the bedroom, attacking his entire body with their flames. His groans woke Nattie with a start. Fumbling in the dark, she reached for the bed lamp, shielding her eyes while they adjusted to the light. When she looked over at Jeed, all she could say was, "Oh no." With her typical quietness and calm, she began to dress herself. It finally dawned on Jeed to look down at himself. His whole body resembled a road atlas, hives covering him from head to foot. Red dots appeared like cities on his mapped body, with blotches covering areas where he had previously worn clothing tight against the skin. His entire crotch blazed crimson, making it look as if he were sporting red jockey shorts. As he stared at the unbelievable sight, his awareness heightened, causing him to feel the pulsing heat of the hives traveling down his back and around his anus.

"Oh God," he groaned. "You taking me to the emergency room?"

"Yes" was all Nattie could choke out, her lips pursed together. Worry wore at her face, which began to worry Jeed. Her work at the hospital had presented her with all kinds of sights that most people could not endure. Sometimes she was called to the ER or to hospital beds when patients looked their worst. She had learned to maintain calm in situations like this. But this was her beloved Jeed, and composure was not easy to come by. "You'd better try and put a bathrobe on," she offered after swallowing the lump in her throat. "You sure can't wear clothing."

Jeed rolled out of bed finding it hard to keep his balance. The fire creatures must have done something to him besides paint him in red. A ringing filled his ears as he tried to get his bearings. Where were the fire beings? Had they left? Buzzing replaced the ringing as a coldness began to replace the heat. Nattie ran over to catch him before he passed out, bracing him with her diminutive frame.

Not a word was spoken on the way to the hospital. At 3 a.m. they entered the sleepy ER. A loony giggle emerged from Jeed's lips as he realized his walk resembled a robot being gently tugged by Nattie. After the paperwork hassle, the nurse ushered the red robot to a gurney and laid him down. Taking his temperature was no problem, but Jeed objected to the blood pressure cuff, his arms covered with itchy red welts.

When the ER doctor arrived, he simply stared at the sight before him. "What did you do?" he asked as if amused, pressing his index finger against several of the reddest welts. The chest ooze had transformed into translucent orange scabs at this point. The puzzled doctor tapped on the largest of the scabs, wondering why they looked like plastic.

"I didn't do anything. It just happened. It feels like poison oak but it isn't," Jeed mumbled, wondering why he was having to explain.

31

After a few more unanswerable questions and pokes at the red tracing of jockey shorts, the doctor ordered an injection of Demerol.

"I want you to soak in a tub of oat water three times a day if not more."

"What's oat water?"

Explanations and more commands issued forth, but Jeed was already spacing out from the Demerol. Nattie took note of every detail. The rest of that night and off and on the next day, Jeed slept in the bathtub of oat water. He spent the next three days in the tub. He had become the swamp creature, living in brown swamp water, roaming the land only to eat. After the third day, the welts finally receded and healing ensued. The nightmare had ended. Or so he thought.

Three weeks after ridding himself of the hives, the itching and redness started all over again. Instead of awaiting another trip to the emergency room, Jeed decided to see his doctor once again. The man was mystified. The merry-go-round of visits, prescriptions, falling scabs, renewed itching, blisters, weeping, and more visits continued for another year. Exasperated, Jeed started seeing specialists, who proved unable to do any better than his regular doctor. His medicine cabinet began to rival the pharmacy itself. Over the next year, he pursued alternate health care: naturopaths, homeopaths, acupuncturists, herbologists, and chiropractors. Instead of prescription drugs, the bathroom began to overflow with teas, potions, salves, essences, vitamins, minerals, and homeopathic pills. The year after that, it was folk medicine. Jeed lost his job, lost his house, lost his self-respect. He urged Nattie to divorce him and find someone more suitable, more capable of carrying his own weight. And the year after that, Jeed tried anything, but anything, that anyone suggested. He had become the biblical Job, cursed to the point of losing everything. Except Nattie. Not only did she keep them afloat financially, she also prepared meals and did the house cleaning when her beloved could not. Without complaint, she watched their lives slip below the poverty level. When they could not afford the mountain of medicinals nor the replenishing of stained clothes, she began to pressure-cook

Jeed's underwear. Laundry detergent couldn't kill whatever it was in the weeping serum that would soak through his T-shirts and sometimes his shorts. If he dared to wear laundered skivvies, the skin eruptions would return overnight. Theirs was a life of the cursed.

Unable to wear certain clothing or to endure the stares of the public, Jeed became a recluse. Using his skills as a computer scientist, along with his love of music, he started his own little cottage business in the computer production of sheet music. Because the market for his skills lay elsewhere, the two of them moved to the Portland area of Oregon. Nattie was able to find a new job as a phlebotomist at University Hospital. Jeed set up computer production in their apartment bedroom, and the two found themselves able to get by. But the forces that had brought such hardship would not leave him alone.

"Nattie?" Jeed whispered. She'd had a hard day at work and was just about to doze off.

"What?" She turned, knowing his tone of voice meant they needed to talk about something. Which usually meant bad news.

"After you left this morning, something very weird happened."

"What about our lives isn't weird?" she joked.

"Something appeared in the room." He let the silence linger.

"You still taking that strange herbal tea?" She was afraid to get serious. There had already been too much seriousness in their lives.

"You mean that orange stuff? Nahh. Didn't do anything except give me diarrhea. Seriously though. This vision of small flashing lights filled the whole corner of the bedroom over there." He pointed to the only free space left. "It had a kind of form to it."

"What kind of form?"

"Well, at first I thought it was like a living Christmas tree, but it had arms. Didn't stay very long, but I could hear this music just before it disappeared. Sounded like trumpets in the distance."

"You've been working rather long hours on your songbook project lately. You came to bed after I fell asleep the night before. Must have been after midnight." Propping herself up on an elbow, she gazed at him with concern. Was he starting to lose it? Was this a nail in the coffin of their Job-like lives? Or had their bizarre life just gotten more bizarre?

"I don't think that's it," he spoke softly, staring beyond the distance of their apartment walls. "After it left, the itching stopped for quite a while. I almost believed this disease had gone." Had he gone over the edge? Had he wished to rid himself of his curse so badly that he was conjuring up singing telegrams? She lay her head on his warm belly, saying nothing. Whatever it was, they would somehow deal with it.

Three nights later, the two of them were sitting in front of the TV, as they liked to do after Nattie cam home from work. While she went to get dinner out of the oven, Jeed began channel surfing. The clicking of the remote ceased as he decided to see what the latest outrage might be on the community access channel. Some middle-aged man with a Brillo pad hairdo was taking callers and talking with his eyes closed. The announcer said the gentleman was channeling the entity Maitreya. Jeed chuckled. He loved the surprises that could show up on the local channel. Portland was such a bag of mixed nuts. But as he began to listen to the phone calls and the responses, he grew curious. The channeler's answers surprised the callers with their accuracy, often bringing forth squeals of embarrassed laughter. *Is this guy for real?* Jeed thought to himself. He turned the volume up to listen to a few more calls. Just as Nattie was placing the plates on the coffee table, Jeed decided, *Why not?* His life was beyond weird already; a little weirder wouldn't matter. Much to his surprise, Jeed rang through on the first try, in spite of the announcer's warning that the switchboard was lit up.

"Your food's getting cold," Nattie warned.

"Hey, I'm gonna be on TV. Want my autograph?"

"You better hope none of your clients are watching," Nattie teased.

"Are you kidding? I'm almost normal in comparison to some of the outlaws I work with."

She listened as Jeed's voice came over the TV. Grabbing the TV remote, she turned the sound down, and then reached for the VCR remote to begin recording the segment. This would be great fun for later. The two of them would have a good laugh over this.

The last four years had made Jeed both a skeptic as well as daredevil. Thoughts of death had begun tickling his mind. Had not the ecstatic love of the God-Light brought him unfathomable joy? Would it not again? The skeptic in him didn't want the man on TV to be able to even understand the question he was about to ask. So Jeed carefully phrased what he wanted to know in a way that few could guess at: "What is the meaning of my journey into the bardo?" Only those knowledgeable of *The Tibetan Book of the Dead* would even know what the bardo was. Purposefully, Jeed decided not even to specify which of the nine bardos he was talking about.

The channeler, with eyes still closed, didn't hesitate in his response. He began a dissertation on the dance that Jeed had with death. "You have walked between the land of the living and the land of the dead. And you still possess the ability to work with both realms." He discussed further Jeed's hesitancy in letting others know all he had been shown in the land of the dead (the bardo). But what shocked Jeed most was the answer to his second question: "What are my guides trying to tell me?" Hopefully, the guy could explain the living Christmas tree that had appeared in his room.

"You have come to bring new teaching to the Earth," the gentleman stated matter-of-factly. "You have no guides, for you are a guide for others. You walk with the masters but refuse to see them. They endeavor to speak with you but you turn a deaf ear. Do not be afraid. You shall not be alone. That which appeared to you was an angel. It appeared as it did because, on December 15th, you shall be visited by the heavens. An event shall occur which will not only change your life but the lives of everyone around you. This will occur in the city of Seattle. You will leave this area and move there before this date. Maitreya sends you the blessings you need to do what you came here to do."

Nattie's jaw dropped open. The living Christmas tree had been an angel? She looked at Jeed who did not act the least bit pleased. Like a man trying to move his life to another channel, he pointed the remote at the TV and shut it off. Without a word, he hung up the phone, picked up his plate and silently picked at the food. Nattie stopped the VCR and rewound the tape. This was too fun not to see again. What a way to end a long day at work.

"The guy's crazy," Jeed mumbled. "There is no chance in hell we're moving to Seattle. After getting a lucrative contract with Simon & Schuster to produce this set of songbooks, there is no way we're leaving here. I've got five employees I subcontract with here. The guy's obviously a fake. No chance in hell." He continued to pick at his food as if it had been invaded by bugs.

"Well," Nattie offered, "December *is* nine months away. It's only March. Who knows what could happen?" Nattie knew what was irking Jeed. The line about doing what he came here to do sounded just a little too much like the line the God-Light had said to Jeed when he was a boy. Had that time arrived? Had an angel actually shown up to try and tell Jeed, with Jeed not wanting to hear?

"It's just not going to happen, Nattie. This is the first time in four years we've had extra money to live on. There's no way we're leaving Portland. No way."

That September, Jeed had to look elsewhere for talent to finish the songbooks contract. And the only place he could contract the special talent he needed was — you guessed it — Seattle. The two of them packed their belongings and found a nice townhouse to rent just north of Seattle. For the first time in years, Nattie didn't feel the pressure of immediately finding a job. Had the trials of the past years finally come to an end? December 15 was not far away.

In November, business had slowed to the point where Jeed and Nattie could actually enjoy themselves — go see a movie, take ferry trips to the San Juan Islands, make new friends. At a gathering of eco-spirituality folks on Whidbey Island, Jeed met a woman who told him about a famous dermapathologist at the University of Washington, his alma mater. Her nephew had gone to see the physician because of a rare skin disease, which the doctor had cleared up. The only problem was that the doctor had a waiting list of one to two years. After hearing of some of Jeed's problems, she scribbled down the name of the dermapathologist and encouraged Jeed to make a call to his office up on Capitol Hill — or "Pill Hill," as it is more affectionately known. A week passed before he could muster enough forgiveness toward the medical profession to give the "best dermapathologist west of the Mississippi" a call.

The receptionist had a sweet childlike voice, not unlike Wanda Wanda from *Romper Room*. She listened attentively, asking pertinent questions about Jeed's history of suffering. "Well, it just so happens we had a cancellation about twenty minutes ago. This lady made the appointment over a year ago. If you'd like to take the canceled appointment, I can get you in two days from today. Can you come on such short notice?"

What luck! Jeed thought to himself. Trying not to sound like someone who'd just discovered gold, he immediately snatched the appointment. He couldn't believe his good fortune. What an opportunity. To finally meet someone who might be able to put an end to his misery. As the day approached, the rash began to abate, as if trying to escape its forthcoming executioner. Jeed became concerned the prominent physician would not be able to appreciate the severity of the condition, with no orange plastic-looking scabs or swarms of tiny blisters or itching red welts marching across his chest.

After waiting forty-five minutes in the waiting room, the moment arrived. Jeed bared his chest and told his story while the sagacious specialist examined what remained of the ongoing infection. "I believe you have ..." Jeed tried to commit the diagnosis to memory but only remembered "subdermal something-or-other something-or-other." *God, why did the name have to be twenty syllables long?* "If I have to, I'll put the full forces of the University Research Center behind finding a solution. Don't worry. We'll get to the bottom of this." Jeed nearly tripped getting into the elevator, he was so euphoric. Before he could start his car, he wept openly, letting go of the years of emotional chaos, his hand grasping a fistful of prescriptions. Hope rested in his grip. He would return in a week.

A few days later, the infection had worsened to such a point that Jeed made an emergency call to the doctor's office. Arrangements were made to come in the next day. No matter what the well-intentioned specialist did over the next few weeks, the blistering, rashes, and oozing defied him. Finally, after another round of prescriptions and failures, the stymied doctor sat down with Jeed and proclaimed, "What you have is incurable. You will have this the rest of your life. I have seen situations like this before. You will have to take steroids for the rest of your life." Anger began to boil up in Jeed. All this time and all this money only to be given what felt like a death sentence. Questions poured out of him as he tried to understand why the white flag was being waved: What would the steroids do to his body? What about the biopsy that had been talked about earlier? How much would this cost financially and healthwise? Was there really no hope?

The dearth of answers left Jeed starving for a reason to trust the doctor's findings. As he marched down the hallway toward the elevator he wanted to hit something, blame somebody, scream until his voice gave out. But all he could do was push the down button. *Going down*, he heard in his head. *The descent into hell*. He had entered Dante's *Inferno*. *Ironic*, he thought, *ironic that it would all come to this*. Why had it taken modern medicine so long to give him this edict? This physician was supposed to be the best. Why did it take him a month of experimentation to ultimately conclude that the disease was incurable? *I'm no fuckin' lab rat*. The elevator door finally opened. Vacant. How appropriate. Never had Jeed felt so alone, so much like a helpless animal trying to escape the maze of hallways and doorways leading to nothing.

As the elevator descended, Jeed's emotions rose. Tears began to escape his tightly shut eyes. He had already witnessed what steroids had done to his body. This was not a long-term solution. As the elevator came to a jolting stop, he remembered a promise he had made to himself. It had been three years ago, after reading Dr. Brian Weiss's book *Many Lives, Many Masters*. In the book, Weiss confesses that his original intent in researching the book was to debunk what was then called "the new psychology" around past-life regression, which uses hypnosis. Instead of disproving the phenomenon, Weiss ended up becoming one of the strongest proponents of this new tool into human consciousness. The author had written about case studies comparable to Jeed's — apparently hopeless health situations — except Weiss found cures by finding causes from other lifetimes. Jeed had made a promise to himself at that time that if he were ever confronted by the prospect of his own condition being hopeless, he would find someone like Brian Weiss who was well grounded in this new psychology.

Over the next four days, Jeed became a madman tearing through articles, library references, New Age newspapers, and references to any psychotherapist whose skills included the new psychology. Finally, one name emerged from his pile of research: Larry Deherrera, Ph.D., and his credentials were impressive. His background in classical psychotherapy balanced well with his forays into the controversial field of past-life regression. Modern psychology had orphaned this new child, not understanding nor attempting to support its growing number of unexplainable successes. Before placing a phone call, Jeed did further research to make sure his time and money would not be wasted one more time by a member of the healthcare profession. Deherrera looked good.

No receptionist answered the call. A phone message would have to be left. Jeed pondered whether to hang up but left a quick message telling of his plight. Within an hour Dr. Deherrera returned the phone call. He introduced himself most cordially and then got to the point.

"Can you give me a brief history of what has happened?" the conversation began. How many times had Jeed told his pathetic history? But one more wouldn't hurt if this man could offer a solution. At the end of Jeed's monologue, silence hung on the line, and with carefully chosen words the therapist responded, "I'm booked up. I'm not taking anymore clients at this time." A ton of bricks hit Jeed. All this effort for nothing? "However, truthfully, I'm very interested in your case. I don't normally do this. But I keep dates open for my current clients in case of emergencies. I'm willing to let you take the last client slot. The only date I have open is December 15th."

Jeed went numb, not even hearing himself mumble, "Holy shit."

"Excuse me?"

"Uhh, nothing. Never mind. Did you say December 15th?"

"Yes, it's the only slot I have available."

"I'll take it," Jeed said, noticing that his heart was pounding like a sledgehammer. "I'll take it. Thank you. Thank you so much."

Chapter Three

THE SETUP

As Jeed gazed across the dancing waters of the Skykomish River, he had only one thing on his mind: December 15 was one week away. The snow-speckled Cascade Mountains rose sharply above the wild alpine river. Chris, Jeed's best friend, had finished his prayer to the river. The Skykomish comforted him like an old friend. Not having been dammed, her north fork still flowed wildly, sometimes raging with temperamental flooding, the result of logging the steep slopes flanking her. Helicopters had been used to remove mature-growth forest. Whenever the bare slopes could not hold the heavy rains or melting snow, the Skykomish would crash against her banks trying to grab at the mountain homes along her shores as if to warn humanity of its foolishness. A giant spruce clung precariously to the shore where Chris sat. One day the Skykomish would come for this magnificent tree if humanity did not change its ways.

Chris glanced over at Jeed, who hadn't moved for almost an hour. He weighed his timing before speaking. "We're never going to get a

Christmas tree cut if we don't do something before dark falls."

"Uh, oh. Yeah. Sorry, Chris. I seem to have a lot on my mind." This time they had decided not to bring Chris's two boys. Chris could tell Jeed was not himself. "You said you already had one picked out?" The two had great respect for this piece of property. Not only was it a spiritual haven, it also was their favorite place to come to hike or fish or spend the night in the shack the two of them had designed and built. Naturally, the structure stood as a mathematical marvel, and had become one of the seven gossiped-about wonders of the town of Index and the surrounding area. Jeed had designed the entire structure on his computer to maximize the space yet fit within the strictures of the building codes so that no inspections or permits would be needed. Chris, a master craftsman in his own right, complemented Jeed's work, having prefabbed the entire framework before carting it up to the property, where they pieced the two-story skeleton together. Because vandalism was a problem with vacation cabins in the area, Chris had managed to build the structure so that no access was visible whenever they locked it up. No windows, no doors, nothing was visible as the corrugated steel exterior folded into a metallic monolith of armor. Only a snorkel of stove pipe emerged from the edifice once they had locked it up. Whenever they left, they always joked about leaving behind Fort Knox.

"So what's going on?" asked Chris. "You've hardly spoken a word since we left Seattle."

"Nothing. Just unwinding from finishing the songbook project." Chris and Jeed had met during Jeed's first music venture while Jeed was a graduate student at the University of Washington. Chris could do things with a guitar that made your ears want to dance. The two of them had collaborated on several songs together, Jeed being the wordsmith. However, only one of their joint efforts had been picked up by a major publisher. Chris was musically ahead of his time. Then again, Chris was ahead of his time in more ways than music.

After trudging through the wet underbrush, they had arrived at the tree that would adorn Jeed's townhouse. Chris couldn't handle a live tree in his house because of allergies. Since Jeed had moved to

Seattle once again, the two had decided to hunt for a tree on the property. But not just any tree could be cut. It had to be a tree in an overpopulated area, so as not to interfere with the balance of the land. After Jeed had rested his hands on the tree to thank it for giving up its life for the joy of the season, Chris revved up the chainsaw and sliced through the trunk in a matter of seconds. "I'd like to ask you something," Chris said, laying the fir on its side.

"What's that?" For years, Jeed's favorite times had been these in-depth conversations with Chris. How long had they known each other? Fifteen, going on twenty years? Where had the time gone? It seemed more like months to Jeed since those days of Vietnam and student protests, and weeks since he'd played tag with Josh and Paul, Chris's two sons.

"You're a smart guy," Chris grinned. He had always seen himself as less than who he was because of forgoing college. "You've studied different cultures and we've talked about how our world needs to change. Well, I want something better for my sons, Jeed." Most parents think their kids are special in one way or another, but Chris's two boys constantly stood out from the crowd. Little did either man know that these two young men would be part of the vanguard of what later would be called the arrival of the Indigos. The term would be coined ten years into the future by authors Lee Carroll and Jan Tober in their book *The Indigo Children: The New Kids Have Arrived*. In an interview conducted by Jan with Nancy Ann Tappe, the term would take off and create discussion around the world about the "new kids." Many ideas would come forth from varied interests offering many different definitions. But the bottom line would be that children with a whole different slant on life were coming forward. Neither Chris nor Jeed were aware of what they were about to become a part of.

"Chris, you've always wanted something better for your sons. What's so different about now?" Even though the two men were the same age, Chris looked years older. His five-foot-seven frame carried a lot of weight other than his own. Thinning hair, graying around the temples, betrayed the years he had played father figure to his five younger brothers. The second youngest, Frank, had been closest to Chris. Frank's suicide over being gay in an intolerant, often hateful, world had taken a severe toll on Chris. The death had stabbed Chris in the heart. What kind of world could not accept such a genuinely loving and gentle being? Frank simply could not live around hate or bigotry nor could he keep his love hidden love. Chris wanted to make sure his own sons could either withstand or change such a world, which had taken Frank from them all.

"Paul is about to get his driver's license and is about to move into manhood. I'd like him to have some sense of his own manhood, some sense of who he is before he faces a world I helped to make."

Chris had survived the Vietnam War in a way that few could. He had turned the entire war into a joke while serving in Southeast Asia. If he wasn't singing protest songs about protest songs, he was strumming tunes that lifted the hearts of those around him. When music wasn't his muse, his pranks were — sometimes to the point of legend. He had survived horror with humor, and he had taught his sons how not to fear looking ridiculous. They had grown up getting used to seeing Dad hanging a spoon off his nose in a restaurant because of slow service. Or balancing the salt shaker on top of his head to get the attention of an overworked waitress. Or taking straws out of his drinks and sticking them up his nose to the complete embarrassment of his wife, Jane. For Chris, survival by humor was not enough any more, not as a legacy for his gifted sons. It was time to set the ridiculous aside and address the sublime.

As the two dragged the blessed tree to Chris's van, Jeed thought about his own initial encounter with manhood and that of his friends. Frankly, he wasn't sure he was in a position to offer any advice. He wasn't sure he had embraced his own manhood. And wasn't Chris himself a Peter Pan figure in many ways? Even after the war? Didn't they need to look at themselves before trying to initiate young Paul into manhood? What was manhood, after all?

Chris began singing Christmas carols as they hauled the tree into the back of the van. But not ordinary Christmas carols: "Jingle Bells, Shotgun Shells," "I'm Dreaming of a Warm Ski Mask," "All I Want for Christmas Is My Two Flat Feet." As they slowly wheeled the van down the gravel road through the tunnel of firs and cedars, Jeed turned to Chris with a smile. "Are you sure it's Paul you want to usher into manhood?"

Chapter four

THE VISITOR

*D*ecember 15 had finally arrived. The words of the trance channeler played back in Jeed's mind: *You shall be visited by the heavens. An event shall occur which will not only change your life but the lives of everyone around you.*

So many questions ran through Jeed's head. What could all this possibly mean? Would Dehererra prove to be just another washout? Or would the prophecy of the TV channeler prove correct? He was about to find out.

Dehererra greeted him with a sturdy handshake. Confidence shone from his bearded face. Jeed could not help but size the man up, as if it would make any difference. His clothes looked as though they had fallen on him by accident — not crumpled but not prim either. Comfortable on his doughlike body. His dark-framed glasses accentuated intense eyes, eyes that could perhaps see what others could not. "Welcome. Make yourself comfortable," the soothing voice said, an open hand extended toward an overstuffed recliner.

Jeed eased himself into the lounger more like an inmate trying to ease himself into an electric chair. "What can I do for you?"

Jeed proceeded through his litany of horrors and hopes. After spending four years of failure with every health-care profession known to humankind, he stated up front that he wanted a clear definition of boundaries and expectations. Larry (as Dr. Deherrera insisted Jeed call him) smiled with recognition: this was not only no ordinary story, this also was no ordinary man. "If the hypnosis works," Jeed said, "which I don't think it will, since it hasn't before, I want everything recorded."

"So you don't think you can be hypnotized?" Larry didn't wait for an answer. "Everyone can experience hypnosis at some level or another. For some, it's deep and heavy, while for others it can be light and almost dreamlike. We can work from either level. You will have control no matter what level we operate from. There's nothing to be afraid of. You can't be asked to do anything against your will." Jeed relaxed a bit. "And as far as recording goes, I've found that clients have a much more difficult time searching through the tape than they do their own memory. Sessions can last a long time, even span days or weeks of time. I'll give you a suggestion that will allow you to remember everything. But if you'd rather have everything taped, we can." Jeed thought Larry had made a good point.

"If there is a chance to enter the bardo either before a birth or after a death, I'd like to go there. I believe it is there where information can be accessed about purpose, cause, and destiny. I'd like to know my purpose for being here, the reason why I've had to go through all this mess." Larry asked Jeed what his definition of the bardo was, just so the two of them might be operating on the same page. "Well, as I know it from *The Tibetan Book of the Dead*, it is a state or place of consciousness between death and the next life, this world and the Otherworld. Typically, it is a place where we evaluate our own lives after death, or prepare our statement of purpose before birth. I want to know why I've been put through this torture, and what I am supposed to do in this life to turn things around." For a long time, Jeed had felt spiritually adrift and in search of something. Though he had been active in a religious sense, having spent a year in the seminary, religion was becoming less and less spiritual to him.

From a professional standpoint, part of what Jeed wanted from Larry was a commitment. Having tried therapy before, Jeed had walked away after one session, enraged by the antics of the therapist. The session had left him convinced that the therapist needed help more than Jeed did. "If possible, I'd like to be able to schedule future sessions to last for as long as I want. I'll pay for the extra time, but I don't want to feel like I'm sitting on an hourglass. I would also like to schedule future sessions for as often as I want — your schedule permitting, of course."

Larry waited until Jeed had exhausted his concerns and needs, and then simply agreed. *This is too easy*, Jeed thought. *Why didn't I think of this a long time ago?* A sigh of relief escaped him. He basked in the surrounding sense of safety and integrity. Larry was a human being as well as a professional. Time to begin.

"I'd like to start with hypnosis," Larry said, "because one way or another, it will tell us what direction will be needed." Using standard techniques to get Jeed into his subconscious, Larry discovered that no matter what he tried, his patient ended up in a void, a dark emptiness, or outer space. The therapist's brow scrunched up with genuine concern and caring. Why was Jeed fighting this? Hypnosis would have to be abandoned for now. After making sure his patient was comfortable and back in a place of full consciousness, the two of them decided that traditional psychotherapy should be tried for a while to see if there was anything of a psychological nature that needed addressing, that might be blocking the hypnosis. Larry suggested that Jeed keep a journal of his dreams and any unusual events throughout the course of therapy. The two scheduled a three-hour session for the next appointment.

Within a few hours of leaving Dehererra's office, Jeed had to sit down and write the first entry. His world had once again entered the realm of the unexplainable:

December 15 (actual event)

After leaving Larry's office, I was taking a Christmas package to the UPS mail station. On the way I was aware of disparate parts of my persona. Had the hypnosis effort triggered this? Within me lurked an apparent need to seem or appear strong when in actuality I needed someone with whom I could be weak. If I were strong, people would not hurt me, or try to hurt me at least. Indeed, they would even look up to me or honor me. But in reality there existed another part of me, an undercurrent of wanting to trust people enough so I could be weak with them. When I arrived at the mail station, I started to fill out the mailing form, first writing my return address. But as I started filling in the ship-to address, I once again became aware of the two separate parts of my personality. It was as if I were coexisting in two levels of consciousness. As one level filled out the form, the other part contemplated my own happiness, or lack thereof. It was as if part of me stood outside my body, watching me. When I looked down at the form, I realized I had written my own address as the ship-to address. I ripped up the form and got another. I then switched back to the other level of awareness and began filling out the form again. Once again, I filled in my own address as the ship-to address. What was going on? On the third try, I managed to stop myself on the first line of the ship-to address, for I again had tried to write my own name as the recipient of the gift. After scribbling out my own name, I forcefully wrote the name of the person I wanted to ship the present to. But on the next line I had to stop again, for I had started to write my own house address. Scribbling out the house number, I again forced myself to slowly write the actual address of where the gift was to be sent. This happened on each and every line, including city, state, and even the zip code. It was as if I were determined to subconsciously send the present to myself. What a bizarre feeling.

Jeed's personal life went on hold after this. The UPS episode so rattled him that he allowed nothing to get in the way of his new adventure with Dehererra. The dreams he wrote down for the next two weeks were like guideposts. Their sessions were spirited and candid; a sense of respect developed between the two. At a critical point in one of their three-hour sessions, Larry just stopped talking, the most pleasant grin spreading across his face. "What?" Jeed demanded, smiling back. The two sat there for a few minutes as if in suspended animation.

"You know, Jeed, you really are a good psychologist." Jeed's eyes rolled. "No, I mean it. You really are very good. I've been in this profession a long time, and I would know. You're working very hard at this, truly. But why not give it a rest? Why not let me be the psychologist for you? Let me be the therapist. Relax and let this happen." Jeed sat there stunned. He wasn't sure whether to be flattered or offended, pleased or embarrassed. Something major shifted in him at that moment. The request from Larry so jarred him that they decided to end the session early, the first time that had ever happened.

That night, a dream came to Jeed which he entered into his journal — one of many since December 15 that seemed to speak to him.

December 27 (dream fragment)

A giant wave rose up from the sea in front of me. I and others stood along a cliff lining the shore. The wave crashed and began to inundate the coastland. As the wave continued to move in, it drowned many people but didn't pass over a wall of stacked wood which had been erected by many of the people. This was a huge wall of wood, and I was standing on top of the stacked wood. The wall must have been 100 to 200 feet high and about 50 feet thick. The water seeped through the wall of split logs into a small valley but the water didn't hurt anyone there. The wave continued to sweep along the wall of wood toward me and came up against a rock peak which I was now hanging onto. The sea rose to my waist and then receded. The name of the peak I was hanging onto was named St. James Peak. (I have had another dream with the name St. James in it. It was a dream in which a ghostly figure came out of a wall socket and took the shape of a person I once knew. The entity began arguing with itself as to what its name was. "I am King James the Lesser. No, I am King James the Greater." There were two apostles named James the Lesser and James the Greater.)

The dream seemed to reference both the drowning during Jeed's childhood and the reluctance he had in fully embracing what the God-Light implied he came here to do. The dream also pointed to the wall Jeed had erected, which Larry had not been able to penetrate, impeding his efforts to bring Jeed to a place of healing. Larry could see the consistent message in the series of dreams, which indicated that Jeed was suppressing a part of himself that he didn't want anyone to know about, including himself. The wall allowed no one onto his spiritual mountain, stopping even the sea of consciousness trying to wash him of his self-made problems. The fact that the sea had stopped at Jeed's waist indicated that the problems might be subconsciously sexual in nature. The dream also indicated that Jeed used his intellect and his mind to hold onto his self-made world, creating an almost schizophrenic approach to life, half of him hiding in the subconscious, half of him dwelling in the conscious, barely holding on. Larry understood that when someone expends as much effort as Jeed had in keeping part of himself a secret — even from himself — that someone will require a near flood of input or major shift of consciousness to overcome such a wall.

The next day, Larry and Jeed got into a confrontation at the start of the session. "I have to be honest with you, Jeed. We've been examining your past and your present, your issues and your hopes, and I have to tell you that as psychotherapist I honestly don't think there is anything wrong with you. There is no pathology here, no mental illness. I've pretty much used all my skills in trying to assist you."

"I'm not sure you've done enough, tried hard enough," Jeed countered, anger beginning to show on his face. Was he about to be disappointed one more time? "All of the options haven't been exhausted." Odd that the client would be telling the therapist how to do his job, but Jeed had spent years researching healthcare, including mental health. He had grown quite fond of Larry and even more impressed with his skills. Their long hours together had opened personal horizons for Jeed he had never considered, never expected. Was it all over?

"And what more would you have me do?" Larry asked calmly, not unlike a cougar looking completely relaxed before it pounces.

Jeed stared at the analyst pointblank, and blurted out a one-word response. "Hypnosis!" The cougar pounced.

"I was just waiting for you to tell me when you were ready." A knowing smile crept across Larry's countenance. The wall had been breached.

"Well, I was waiting for you to tell me when you were ready, too. Let's get on with this." Jeed's body almost shook with nervousness about what might or might not happen. After what seemed like an eternity of relaxing and focusing techniques, Larry finally was able to get Jeed to slip into a subconscious state.

Jeed's mind moved into three states of awareness, rapt in total fascination as he communed with all three parts of himself. The conscious self sat over on a bluff, watching everything going on. It sent a telepathic message to Jeed, letting him know it would carefully oversee all that would happen. If anything didn't seem right, it would intervene and end the session immediately. The subconscious self felt like a blank movie screen exuding a sense of total peace and cooperation. Then there was the superconscious self, which immediately began sending information at a subliminal level, which Jeed could not understand. The message it was conveying seemed to be trying to keep Jeed calm in preparation for what was about to unfold. The information had no origin, appearing out of what could only be described as hyperspace. Then Larry spoke the sentence that would change Jeed's life forever.

"Let us go to the cause of this disease."

As if in some kind of Disneyland pavilion, symbols of all kinds started swirling around Jeed. He couldn't make sense out of any of them, seeing quick flashes of the sparkling lights that had invaded his bedroom nine months ago. With every skill at his means, Larry tried to clear the clutter and bring into clarity what the mind was trying to understand. Finally, Jeed saw a pair of feet in clear focus. With patience and fortitude, Larry brought the picture into full view. A sixteen-year-old boy sat in stocks, his feet clamped with chains. Larry's experience immediately determined that Jeed most likely was witnessing a past life. What was he doing in what appeared to be colonial America? Keenly, he began uncovering pieces of information that might reveal what had caused the skin disease.

The town fathers had shackled the boy for repeated sexual offenses. He had been caught playing with himself time and again by relatives. Jeed's conscious self shook its head, almost laughing. This was a crime? The boy had been rebellious, clever, and outspoken about the role of the self-righteous dictating what was and was not a sin. The religious figures of the town insisted that the boy had been influenced by the Devil, and the Devil needed to be driven from him. The boy would eventually die for his stubbornness, his refusal to toe the line.

Larry decided not to spend too much time with this past life and moved on. It didn't seem to address the cause of the disease — or did it? He needed more information. After a pause, he suggested that they move on to whatever else might be at the source of the incurable disease, and Jeed found himself in another era. He didn't know how he knew, but he could see himself in seventeenth- or eighteenth-century France. Before him loomed a great church, which he realized he had built. The daring design stood as an architectural marvel, and he was quite proud of it. Once again, Larry guided Jeed through part of that life and then moved on to two other lives, looking for the key to Jeed's disease. What Larry was looking for didn't stand out, so he returned to the lifetime in France. This time, Larry led Jeed in intimate detail through a life of tragedy, like the other two lifetimes they had visited. It appeared that Jeed loved to stir up controversy, and this lifetime stood out poignantly in that regard. The information coming forward revealed that Jeed had been an architect of great repute, with many apprentices in his charge. The architect had decided to use his fame to take on the Church itself. For he had been terribly upset at how the Church had taken upon itself the right to define aspects of love as perverted or sinful. Sex raged against the spirit, the carnal being the enemy of the soul. The architect believed that God truly was love. How could any aspect of love be wrong or perverted or sinful? It was like trying to say that part of God is sinful. The whole notion was preposterous.

While building this latest church, the architect had found his life's love, a woman of incredible beauty and tenderness. Her father was the mayor of the city and in league with the local religious authorities as to how the city was governed. The couple was to be wed in the very church the architect had constructed. This would be a legacy to love, a legacy to intellect over superstition, a legacy to spirituality over politics. But the Fates would intervene. For the architect had built a statement into the architecture of which no one knew, except his most trusted students. Such architectural statements were not uncommon, especially with certain schools such as that led by the architect. In this case, the architect had built angelic gargoyles as gutter spouts along the roof line. In broad daylight, they looked over the church grounds with artistic beauty, prominent in their contrast to the typical griffin or gremlin gargoyles of other churches. But on one particular summer night, a thunderstorm quickly passed over, leaving torrents of water and a full moon in its wake. Water poured off the church while the full moon highlighted the architect's hidden statement. From the plaza below, a crowd began to gather, heads craned upward, erupting into bawdy laughter. The silhouettes of the angels no longer appeared so angelic. Their wings no longer shone like wings but as scrotums to phallic extensions, as if they were taking a collective whiz off the church roof. The pouring rain, combined with the moonlight, revealed to the gathering townspeople the gargoyles' true intentions — a statement of satire: God pissing on a worldly Church which dared to label any aspect of love as evil. Love can never be evil. Love is the very essence of God in every form and facet. It is only the small-mindedness of men that can create evil from that which is sacred.

The master builder's architectural joke was not taken kindly by the city fathers, to say nothing of the bishop or the Church fathers. They proclaimed the architect "shunned," ostracized, never to work again, never to be allowed on sacred ground for the rest of his days. His bride-to-be found herself spirited away by her embarrassed father, never to see her fiancé again. There would be no wedding. Rather than fight fire with fire, the architect retreated into despair, abandoning his school of followers ready to join him in open rebellion. Rather than become the city's rebel, he became the town drunk. Once the champion of innovative and rebellious young architects throughout France, his name became synonymous with shame.

One dark night, while in a drunken stupor, the horse the architect was riding spooked at his rider's retching. The frightened beast, vaulting into the woods, passed too near a tree. A lower limb caught the drunk neck high, knocking him off the horse, breaking his sorry neck in the process. His body rolled down the incline into the roadside ravine. Paralyzed, he lay near-dead, unable to move. Those who found him by lantern light retrieved the priest, who pronounced the town drunk dead. Because the architect had been ostracized, he could not be buried in hallowed ground. The church groundskeeper retrieved a shovel from the cemetery shed and, at the behest of the curé, covered the body in the ravine with dirt — burying the architect alive.

As Jeed's subconscious self felt the weight of the dirt pressing against his body, his conscious self watched the architect being buried alive, wondering if it should intervene or end the session. But then Larry suggested that the entire scene could be watched from outside the body without experiencing the sensations of death. Jeed felt no panic as the architect began to suffocate. He watched himself die. And, as agreed, the therapist asked the soul to move into the world beyond death: the bardo. "Please describe for me what you are seeing and feeling now," suggested Larry.

"There is golden light everywhere, completely surrounding me. It is so peaceful here, totally peaceful," Jeed responded in dulcet tones. "I feel like I'm floating in love, a total freedom floating through me." The life in France fell away like so much dust blown by a golden breeze.

Larry nodded knowingly. "Let us ask what your purpose is, your life's mission on Earth." It struck Jeed as odd how the question had been phrased. Just as his mind began wondering about the time frame, he suddenly noticed a being of light in the distance, now moving toward him. As it drew nearer, Jeed decided it must be an angel, but he had never seen anything of such extraordinary beauty. The sight so engulfed Jeed with its breathtaking exquisiteness that Larry immediately noticed the change in his client's breathing. He waited. Jeed stared, mesmerized by the brilliant light twenty feet in front of him. The love emanating from the angel struck him with a familiarity, a love he had not known since that day as a boy, lying dead at the bottom of a river, and then taken before the God-Light. The celestial's dazzling light pushed back the golden glow that had once flooded the bardo. As Jeed adjusted to the intensity of the angel's aura, he began to notice two different patterns in its body. It was as if a line had been drawn from its left shoulder to its right hip. The lower portion emitted a silvery mother-of-pearl iridescence from its robe, almost ghostlike. The upper portion of the angel's body shone with rainbows within rainbows of crystalline color rising up from what appeared to be prisms within prisms. The color made the prisms appear as if they contained dimensional openings of irregular shapes, a living cubist painting. As Jeed's eyes moved upward, his mind fought for explanation. For the angel had no features where a face would be. There appeared only fathomless light, bright as the sun. As he stared at the countenance, he became fully aware of what the celestial felt and knew. They had become one. Surreal love overtook him, joy burning inside him like a pyre. No judgment existed. Life could not be separated from death. The being had come to assist Jeed. It spoke.

"Your purpose is as it has always been," it answered in response to Larry's question. "To lift up the lowly, to give strength to the weak, to bring justice to those suffering injustice. It is the same in this lifetime as it has been in every lifetime." Jeed noticed his conscious self, still sitting on the side, smiling in awe. Flashes of incredible awareness began to fill him. For as the angel spoke, it spoke on three different levels. At the first level, the words he had just heard also came through his own voice. Larry could hear these words, not knowing it was the angel speaking through Jeed's mouth. The conscious self, the second level, wondered whether Larry could see the angel, imagining he could not. Otherwise, why use Jeed's voice? The conscious self already was beginning to analyze the consequences of what the angel implied in stating that the purpose was the same in this lifetime as it had been in every lifetime. In human terms, this statement departed from the expected norm. Humans face different purposes in different lifetimes. Why would Jeed's lives run counter in this regard? Could it be related to the channeler's statement that Jeed had no guides, that he was himself a guide for others? Was Jeed somehow different from other humans? And if so, why?

The third level at which the angel spoke created a kind of holographic message. Information poured into Jeed's mind like a whole set of encyclopedias. What confounded and stunned Jeed was his ability to be aware of and understand all this knowledge at once. That was until his conscious self began to think about it. As soon as his mind issued forth a thought, the knowledge exploded into fragments, and Jeed could no longer comprehend the totality. Not that the knowledge was lost but as if it had separated into hundreds of books now stored on library shelves. One book at a time could then be referenced, the fragmented knowledge understandable only as a partial of the whole. Immediately he desired to return to the state of understanding the whole, but he could not, regretting he had formed the thought. A telepathic voice now entered his mind, coming from a source unknown. "You are not who you think you are," it said. The conscious self reeled at this and began searching for both the meaning and the source. *What does this mean?* it demanded. *Why are you saying this?* it yearned to know. But only a feeling of a future explanation could be discerned.

Noticing the awe in Jeed's face, Larry decided to press for more information about his client's purpose. "Is there another purpose, another mission?" What immediately appeared in front of Jeed was a large white ball of light, much like a giant pearl of great worth. The great pearl was partially hidden by a gauzelike veil.

"I can see the other purpose," Jeed reported, "but there is a curtain in front of it that keeps me from knowing the purpose."

"Then reach out with your mind and draw the curtain back," Larry countered. Jeed was about to reach out and pull the curtain back when the angel stepped in front of it, prohibiting him.

"I can't," Jeed said. "The angel is standing in front of it."

"Angel?" Larry's voice sounded surprised and worried at the same time. *Where did the angel come from?* he wondered.

"Yes, a beautiful being of light. I think it's an angel."

"What makes you think it's an angel?"

"Well, it is made of great light and has so much love. No wings, though. Its face is featureless, just solid light. I've heard angels sometimes appear that way."

"Ask the angel if it might step aside so that we might see this other purpose or mission."

The angel responded through Jeed's voice, "You may not know this at this time. For if you did, you might misuse it or abuse it. The information is not ready to be made known." Larry shifted in his therapist's chair, suddenly aware the celestial was speaking through Jeed's voice. This disturbed him almost as much as the warning. While Larry's mind searched for the best move to make to help his client, Jeed's third level of consciousness once again went into bliss as another set of encyclopedias stuffed his brain. An entire body of knowledge about the destiny of Earth and its people was suspended before him in magnificent wonder. He understood the fullness of the harmonic revelation until once again a single thought from him exploded the completeness into singularities. He could understand individual strains of information not unlike a strong solo voice singing above an a capella choir in pianissimo.

"I'm going to end the session now," Larry calmly announced. "You will be able to remember everything that has happened. You will feel peaceful and relaxed as I count from ten to one. Ten ... nine ... eight ..."

Jeed's conscious self, sitting on the sidelines, began to yell thoughts of *No, no. Stop! I need to find out more about this angel. I need to find out who sent it, where it came from.*

"Seven ... six ... five. Feeling better, lighter, very refreshed and peaceful ... four ... three ... two ... one. You can open your eyes now."

As Jeed regained full consciousness, staring at the ceiling, he was about to chew Larry out for ending the session. Snapping the recliner to attention, he froze before a word could escape his lips. There, standing off to the left of the therapist stood the angel in all its splendor. Jeed sat breathless. The angel's light blazed even more gloriously than it had under hypnosis.

Puzzled over the look on Jeed's face, Larry asked, "Are you feeling OK?" His client seemed frozen in space. What was he staring at? Larry looked to his right, seeing nothing. "Are you OK?" he asked once again. Words poured from Jeed, but they were not Jeed's words.

"You have sought God in the highest of ways. You have taken the highest of paths." It was the angel's voice, again speaking through Jeed. Larry blanched. "You have sought and found the highest of truths among the wise. But you must also know that God is to be found in the least of these." At another level of consciousness the angel spoke telepathically. "You have been born into a gay body for a Divine reason. And you have run from your purpose for being here." All of a sudden, Jeed realized what "the least of these" meant. Sitting there thunderstruck, the avalanche of realization covered him like a death blow. *I am gay?* For years he had struggled with the thought and repeatedly dismissed it. His past denials crumbled like a giant sandcastle hit by a sea of truth. Breathing ceased as his mind reeled with the repressed memories of lovemaking with a past friend — what the two of them had called "deep friendship." Tears began falling from his eyes like raindrops. Sobs burst forth, catching Larry totally off guard. All Jeed could do was stare in disbelief. *What will Nattie think?* Thirteen years of marriage took on the specter of a great escape. The sobbing rocked him. Years of self-fear and self-judgment erupted in an emotional retching. How many years had he wasted? How could he forgive himself?

Then, a third implosion of mass information hit him. This time, the body of knowledge revealed the true relationship between masculine and feminine. It laid out the hypocritical war between male and female. Centuries of abuse to the Earth — to the feminine, the Goddess, the Gaia — spread before him like a mosaic of tragedy and destruction. But surrounding the past was a bright ring of the future, how the feminine would move back into balance, changing all life, changing the world itself. Even the long persecution of gays and lesbians would come to an end with the realization that nature had ordained the preservation of the androgynous in them. There was spiritual androgyny and physical androgyny. In the future lay the eventual embracing of both masculine and feminine within the spiritual. Within himself lay this state of being, which he had abandoned. The onus of shame caused him to question himself, the thought once again shattering the plenitude before him. Regret upon regret cascaded upon him. He had betrayed his purpose, his calling, his very reason for being here. Despair erupted from him like an awakening volcano. Nasal rheum now joined the river of tears as he wailed like a man who had lost everything. Or had he ever had anything in the first place? All those years of hiding and running from himself. Larry sat mesmerized, helpless to do anything but watch.

The angel caught Jeed's attention as it reached out to touch him with its right hand, sending a great blast of light into him. As it lifted its left arm to the side, its right arm pointed heavenward. The garment of light-within-light hanging from its left arm seemed to hide something behind it. As the angel swept its left arm grandly across its prismed body, a new dimension — a whole new reality — opened up behind where the arm had been. A shock of beatific wonder hit Jeed. There it was once again: the God-Light had returned. The ecstasy of love once again poured forth as it had done so many years ago. Jeed's weeping ceased. Unfathomable forgiveness surrounded and stunned him, an unending, unconditional forgiveness. Unending forgiveness was his for the taking. But a mystery of hesitation held him like chains. No matter how much he tried, Jeed could not embrace the forgiveness. Even though the God-Light had forgiven him, he could not forgive himself. The angel tried to help Jeed understand how simple it was to accept this gift, but even that did not help. Jeed dropped his head, wiping the tears and snot from his face. No, he could not forgive himself. The angel's left arm returned to its former place, hiding the God-Light.

A compassionate voice issued forth from the angel. "You are to tell five people of what has happened here today." Jeed could see images of the five people: Nattie; his best friend, Chris; his music publisher; and two other prominent figures in the world of sacred music and liturgy. "If they will hear you and understand, then the vision of a greater world that you saw shall come to pass." Jeed could see how their free wills, if used in harmony with the will of the Creator, could bring about a great healing to our world. But who would believe what had happened? Who could understand what even Jeed himself could not understand? He looked up at Larry, seeing the confusion in his face.

"Jeed, don't take too much on. You can come back, you know. You don't have to deal with everything now. Take your time."

Jeed's lips pursed. "I know what I have to do." And at the word "do" the angel vanished in a snap, brilliant light instantly surrendering to lamplight. Jeed repeated himself. "I know what I have to do. I'll settle up on my bill now."

Sleep did not come to Jeed that night. He didn't even bother going to bed. His mind seemed as if it were going to explode. Nattie kept asking if anything were wrong. What was he going to say to her? Kind, loving, understanding Nattie. She was one of the five he must tell, but how could he possibly?

The next morning, Nattie shuffled down the stairs to find her beloved still sitting on the couch staring into emptiness. Her silent, caring self simply coasted over next to him and warmed him with her embrace, resting her head on his neck. Jeed began to shake. "Nattie. I have a story to tell you. A long story."

Their lives would never be the same. Exactly a week later, Jeed went to bed with the skin rash erupting on his chest, resigned to having it flare up with the usual tortures. But when he arose the next morning, it was gone. Completely. Never to return. The incurable had somehow been cured.

The angel returned two more times that year, trying to steer Jeed back to his purpose. At Nattie's request, they stayed together for a few more years, leaving Seattle and returning to Portland. Little did Jeed know of the mysterious set of circumstances that awaited him. The heavens would make sure that the downloaded information would not be lost. Over time, Jeed constantly battled within himself as to what should be done with the information he had been given. His life had been turned upside-down, leaving him in disarray and confused as to what direction he should take. How could he make up for lost time? Should he?

Chapter Five

THE CALLING

I've been reading how our society fails to bestow manhood on our sons," said Chris. He and Jeed stood on the back deck of Chris's three-story house, watching the flocks of geese winging across the Seattle sky like a dappled ribbon floating on a breeze. Jeed marveled at how beautiful the view of Puget Sound and the Olympic Mountains could be in early autumn. "Two years ago, we tried to welcome Paul into his manhood by having that little get-together where we made a big deal about his getting his driver's license. Remember how we tried to use that to recognize his coming manhood? Tried to ritualize it? I don't think it really worked. I would like to try something different with Josh." Chris was right. In spite of his and Jeed's good efforts, the ceremony of verbally acknowledging Paul as a man didn't have its intended effect. Paul confessed later that he was actually a bit embarrassed because the whole thing struck him as pretentious. Chris had given Paul two symbols: a salmon tapestry and a miniature Pacific Northwest Native totem pole to serve as mementos of his being accepted as a man. After the acceptance ceremony Paul had been given two choices as to how he might celebrate the occasion: have a sumptuous dinner with the *men*, or take the money that would have gone toward dinner and use it however he wished. He didn't bat an eyelash in deciding. He took the money, bought gas, and drove his buddies all over town. American maleness at its purest: showy, temporal, flashy.

"You helped Malidoma write a book on ritual." Chris's eyes turned and focused on Jeed as he parked himself on one of the handmade benches surrounding the deck. Truthfully, Jeed had learned a great deal working with Malidoma Somé on the book *Ritual: Power, Healing, and Community.* He had learned even more afterwards, studying with the African shaman-priest for a year. But would such cross-cultural mysticism be appropriate for Josh? What neither Jeed nor Chris knew was that Josh represented the beginning of a new kind of consciousness entering into American society. Though constantly thinking himself a misfit through elementary school and into high school, he had begun to understand that he was meant to be different, meant to transcend the norm. His ability to be different showed itself when he began dating his first girlfriend, an young Asian woman. Though a large minority in the Seattle area, Asians still suffered the outrage of white prejudice. Though not "cool" to be seen dating an Asian girl, Josh moved beyond even the larger issue of falling in love with her despite social pressures against it. Instead of remaining the misfit, he moved into a place of leadership and example, respected by most in his high school. Yes, this was the beginning of tearing down old the mores, old patterns, and old restrictions that constantly separate our world. These young men and women, who would later be called Indigos, came to do nothing less than change our world. Would initiation help or hinder such a purpose? The question had serious implications, and Jeed knew it.

For Jeed, the hours spent trying to put Malidoma's African notions into a book written in English proved a tough task. Malidoma's intimate knowledge and workings with the spirit world come from a tradition that has no word for "supernatural." To his people, there is no separation between natural and supernatural. "Nature" includes both realms. Jeed had struggled arduously to describe African indigenous terms in English. The English language simply did not have words that could even come close to some of the concepts of the Dagara of Burkina Faso. The exercise of trying, first, to understand these foreign spiritual beliefs and, second, to come up with language that would explain the unexplainable, proved to be a terrific learning experience for Jeed. From a Christian perspective, parables had been used by Jesus to accomplish such a task, but how does one create a parallel mechanism for a foreign culture's spirituality? Jeed learned patience in working with Malidoma. Sometimes they would spend a half-hour on a single word — like "shaman." In English , the word has become nearly meaningless because it has become a catchall. The meaning can wander from the Native American concept of witch doctor to the current use describing some modern-day psychologists who employ avant-garde techniques. Healers, diviners, medicine men, holy women, and eco-spiritualists often get thrown into that caldron of meaning.

Malidoma Somé describes himself as an African shaman-priest, a medicine man/diviner who also happens to be a professor and scholar holding two Ph.D.'s and three master's degrees. His two doctorates, in political science and literature, were awarded at the Sorbonne in Paris and at Brandeis University in Massachusetts. What an amazing man. He could not only argue philosophy and politics, he could also sit with a sick child on whom medical doctors had given up, and, with cowry shells, herbs, and chanting, return the child to full health. Malidoma had insisted in his meetings with American men that our society is in a state of sickness because we fail to initiate our boys into manhood. Many, if not most, American males still are not initiated into manhood. Jeed had listened time after time as audiences would question Malidoma for packaged answers as to how rituals and initiations ought to occur. Jeed smiled everytime he heard Malidoma's answers. "These matters cannot be thought of as items at a supermarket. You can't just go along an aisle and pick up a ritual, take it to the counter and pay for it. This is the Western way of doing things. And in this case, it is not right. You cannot purchase or make a consumer product out of ritual. You must find your own. You cannot take African ritual and plop it into your lives and make it American ritual."

This, of course, had reminded Jeed of similar protestations by Native American leaders who had accused whites of "playing Indian." Jeed's own father had left a legacy of shame about being part Cherokee; he was ashamed of having "Injun" blood in him. He would rarely talk about the family lineage on that side. Jeed, however, had become quite proud of his Native heritage. But he, too, did not like "playing Injun" with Native rituals. And if he felt uncomfortable with the sacredness, how could whites not feel equally uncomfortable? Jeed had no difficulty taking Malidoma's message to heart.

As the sun began to set, leaving a growing nip in the air, Chris continued the conversation. "I think what we need is to somehow create a ritual. And I think the ritual should be used to receive Josh into his own manhood, like some sort of initiation rite. I've thought a lot about it, Jeed, and I, myself, don't ever really remember feeling there was a single moment that I embraced my manhood, not even during the Vietnam War. Vietnam left me with a feeling of power at times, but I don't remember a single event where I could claim ownership of who I was as a man. In fact, I still feel there is something missing because of the way my father died."

It wasn't enough that Chris's father had been an abusive alcoholic. In the end, he had committed suicide by jumping off one of the interstate overpasses shortly after being caught stealing at a convenience store. He had more than enough money in his pocket to pay for what he had stolen. None of it made any sense. Chris felt he hadn't been given an opportunity to have any kind of closure or reconciliation with his father. The guy simply bailed out.

Suicides had not only impacted Chris's life. Jeed, too, had come from a family steeped in one kind of abuse or another. He, too, had a suicide to remember — that of his younger sister, who, like their mother, had suffered from chronic alcoholism. Both Chris and Jeed knew of the statistic showing an increasing suicide rate among teens. Neither wished to face that tragedy ever again. Whatever was at play in our society that made life not worth living had to be changed. Perhaps their efforts with Josh could be the beginnings of such change. How right they would turn out to be.

Like Chris's father, Jeed's father had been a strange mixture of abuse and cowardice, being either absent from home (out working two jobs) or raging when he was at home. Whenever his tirades and violence turned toward Jeed, the son paid dearly for his membership in the "family." Far too often the father's favorite belt doubled as a whip. In those days, belts about the width of a pencil were popular, the buckles made of chrome-covered metal. Either end of the belt could be used, depending on how raw his father's rage, to lash at Jeed's back and calves, usually to the point of bleeding. If the son dared cry out, the lashing only grew worse.

"What about the way some Native Americans initiated their young men?" Chris suggested. "What about using some part of those rituals?" Jeed knew that Chris was aware of his stance on borrowing from Native ritual. So why had he asked the question anyway? *Probably to force discussion on alternatives*, he thought. *Is he that serious about this?* Jeed wondered.

"Let's go inside. This dampness is chilling my bones. I need to think about this." As they opened the sliding glass door, the warmth of the house welcomed the two friends. Made of solid brick, the house had stood for several decades. The old-fashioned character of it had been comforting over the years. Jeed felt more at home here than any other place he knew. As they sat silently in the living room, Jeed stared at the empty fireplace across the room as he dove into his thoughts.

After Jeed had told the story of the angel and his healing to the five people, only two had remained his friend afterwards: Chris and Nattie. Those five people had been Jeed's closest friends and colleagues. Losing the friendship of the other three had devastated him. His life had turned into total disarray afterward. Nattie had wanted to stay married in spite of Jeed's honesty and conviction that he owed it to himself to no longer live in the closet. The two had moved back to Portland since work in Seattle had dried up. Jeed had struggled with great difficulty about being gay, and eventually decided that he and Nattie needed to split up.

The fact that Chris had remained his best friend meant the world to Jeed. He visited Chris often in Seattle. This was a man he could trust, who deserved support, who did not flinch at the prospect of a gay man initiating his youngest son into manhood. Had not Malidoma intimated that the gatekeepers who helped initiate young men of the Dagara into manhood also were gay? Perhaps there was a reason for this. Perhaps power, which flowed from the feminine, was essential to balance strength, carried by the masculine. Maybe that's why the gatekeepers of the Dagara were revered by the tribe. The Dagara had a reputation in Africa as being the most feared tribe. They were called the "Magic People." And Malidoma had left no doubt that magic played an essential role in Dagara initiations. Could an American boy find magic while entering into manhood? *Find it? Hell, could he survive it?* Jeed wondered. Maybe that's why Chris was pressing so hard. Something in him knew that magic had to happen. Could Jeed take all he knew, even the information from the angel, and create magic in a modern context? He loved his best friend, who dearly loved his son. The risk must be taken — not only for Chris and Josh but for those who might follow.

"There may be merit in looking at the way the ancients ritualized initiation," Jeed confessed. "But I feel we must adapt it to our time and our cultural needs. The ancients were a warrior people. They had to survive not only the challenges of nature but also the demands of hunting and warring with other tribes. I don't believe that is our focus today. Instead of being warriors, I believe we are called to be peacemakers, stewards, or magicians. We are in an age of wonders where science transforms and mystifies. Warrior types may be needed in business, but I believe, for the most part, those who really flourish in our society are those who know themselves, who can transform themselves, and who in turn transform those around them. Our challenges nowadays are no longer hunting and warring and surviving in nature. Instead, we find the worst violence comes from within, the worst challenges come from within.

"So let's see if we can take the ways of the ancient warriors and adapt them for our time, a time of the Magician, the Magus, the Wise Man, the Transformer. Let's see if we can come up with a ritual that will allow Josh to transform from a boy into a man."

Chris's eyes lit up as he began tugging at his mustache. "OK. Well, let's start with the notion that initiations often started by sending the boy out into the woods alone, into nature. In some cases, he stayed there until he killed his first meal or had a vision quest, or he spent several nights with the Elders, performing various tests."

This wasn't the Magician that Jeed had tried to convey. This was the Warrior/Survivor — man against nature. Man needed to stop confronting nature and instead steward nature, come into balance with nature. "Maybe instead of sending him out into nature, we could simply send him on a journey to where he's never been that involves nature." Journeys are about transformation, which is closer to what men need in discovering themselves, changing themselves, balancing themselves. "He's never been on a train or been away by himself. He's always been in your care, under your protection, your supervision. Perhaps we could send him down to Portland where I could meet him, and the ritual could take place out in the Columbia River Gorge. The Gorge is only a half-hour drive from Portland and contains some of the most dramatic naturescapes in the world." The Columbia River, which separates most of Oregon from Washington to the Pacific Ocean, flows through the heart of the Gorge. The walls of mountains and cliffs which line the Columbia form a kind of pipeline where extremes in weather charge through, constantly changing panoramas with wind, rain, sun, and shadow. "There's a place I know of called Beacon Rock, a great place for a ritual, not far from what the Native people called the Bridge of the Gods. The energy there is amazing, as are the surroundings — untamed, wild, yet breathtaking." Indeed, Native American petroglyphs line parts of the Gorge to this day, telling of the legends of the gods who formed this great spiritual landscape. The Multnomah, the Klickitat, the

Clackamas, and the Kalapuya told great legends of the deeds and misdeeds of the gods. The Native legends bespoke the transformations inherent in the struggles of the gods.

"Maybe Paul and I could go with Josh and perform the ritual," Chris said. This is where friendship made it possible to speak from the heart.

"I have to confess to you that I don't think that's a good idea," Jeed said softly. "In essence, what you are saying is that *you* want to initiate Josh into manhood. One of the truths I learned in listening to Malidoma is that a father can never initiate his own son into manhood. At first I didn't agree with him. But after giving it a lot of thought, I believe Malidoma is right. The father is tied to the 'boy.' It is the father and mother who bring the boy through life. How can the boy die to the emerging man when the father and mother have so much invested in the boy? And how can the father truly bring the boy through the threshold of manhood when the father may not be willing to let the boy die? No. I think it has to be someone other than the father. In the indigenous cultures, it was a shaman or an Elder or a group of Elders who took on the responsibility of fostering the boy through the threshold of manhood. Rather than doing the initiation, what about serving as witnesses to the initiation?"

Chris searched within himself to feel out the truth of this. "Yes, that makes sense to me. And I think you would be the right man, Jeed. Josh trusts you. I trust you."

An old feeling crept up Jeed's spine while he considered Chris's suggestion. The feeling came from a time when shadows of June bugs danced upon his bedroom wall. If the truth be told, the source of the uneasy feeling had echoed long before childhood. The words of the angel began to stir within Jeed's thoughts. Chris's suggestion opened certain "books" within the libraries of knowledge the angel had given him. Something in him made him afraid. He shuddered. "Thanks for saying so, Chris. But I'm not so sure. This could be an intense experience which may require a significant investment and personal risk. I'm not sure I can be considered an Elder yet. We're both only forty-seven. Many of the indigenous people thought a man had to be at least fifty before being considered an Elder."

"That may be true," Chris countered, "but I think there is more to this than just age. I consider you a modern-day shaman. You possess gifts which others do not. You understand the ways of other realities. And you have studied with your friend Malidoma, who told you, if I'm not mistaken, that you needed to let out these 'secrets' that dwell within you. I think you would be perfect. You know a lot about ritual. And what's more important, you know a lot about Josh."

Something rumbled around in Jeed as he heard these words, something that agreed. The secrets must be released. But his brain was telling him, *No. Don't do it! Remain hidden.* "Chris, I don't feel comfortable in this role. It's too loaded — a gay man helping a boy move into manhood at a critical time in his development? Something within tells me this won't stop with Josh if I decide to do it. And I don't trust society. Too many will be tempted to make something perverted out of this." There it was. The cathedral architect in France rising from the ashes of an ancient memory. The karma was returning, the purpose for being born staring him in the face once again, only in a different way. Malidoma had told Jeed that men such as he held the mysteries of life, whether welcoming a boy into manhood or welcoming a soul before birth. Even though Malidoma's tribal culture had no word for "gay," they knew those born as gatekeepers were born with special spiritual gifts. In Malidoma's village, his people held up such gatekeepers with great regard. The reason there was no word for "gay" in Dagara culture came from the fact that these spiritually gifted ones, these gays, are not seen as separate nor separated from the fabric of the community. They exist as an essential component.

"I don't know if our society is ready for this. And I don't think I'm ready for it."

"Jeed, it makes no difference to me that you're gay. This really is a matter of carrying gifts and using them. I know your giftedness. I've not only seen it, I've been the beneficiary of it. Manhood isn't a matter of sexual orientation, it's a matter of accepting responsibilities, a matter of creating a better world, a matter of standing before the world and saying, 'I count. I am here to grow in love and knowledge.

I am here to help when needed and to ask for help when in need.' I don't care what society thinks. I think we need to turn this around. It's a matter of changing society itself. One man at a time. Come on. You know I'm right."

Jeed's uneasiness kept him silent for a while. Maybe Chris was right even if it didn't seem right. Were these friends the right people, and was this the right time? Chris had spoken on behalf of his son. But what about what the son thought? Did Josh have a say in this? Was Josh prepared for the forces that could be unleashed upon him? In indigenous societies, the tribal Elders gave the boy little choice. In some cases, they literally kidnapped him from his family. That might be justified in a warrior society, but not in a society of magicians. The sorcerer's apprentice needed to be warned about what he was getting himself into. Magic had to be respected, even in the hands of an apprentice. "You understand, of course, for ritual to be done correctly, the spirit realm must be invited in. And I would have every intention of doing that."

"Josh is no stranger to the spirit world," Chris offered. "I don't think that's a problem. He has witnessed me and Paul in ritual, sharing our spiritual sides with the folk choir at mass, as well as Native American vision quests. Really, I don't see a problem here."

"Then he must be made aware of the potential for his world as he knows it to end. We will invite the mystery of the unknown, which means just about anything could happen. In the Dagara initiations, it is not unusual for an initiate to die in the process of entering his manhood. I'm not saying that's the case here. I'm just saying there are forces at work here which you or Paul or Josh may not be aware of. There is no telling what we may tap into. Once we start this, there is no turning back. When one invites the spirit realm into ordinary reality, very unordinary things can happen."

Chris's mind whirled with memories of some of the strange events that had already occurred because of Jeed's work with angels. Over the last eight years, Jeed had vacationed with Chris's family up in Priest Lake, Idaho, during the month of July. Over the years, Jeed had increasingly opened the minds of Chris's sons to some rather unexplainable phenomena. Josh really believed that Jeed could talk to angels. The first year of the annual trek, Jeed had decided to add a little fun and mystery to the boys' summer. He invented an angelic being named "Jehosephat," who inhabited the island in the middle of the lake. He had taken the boys to the island one evening in Chris's cabin cruiser. The island purportedly held ancient secrets guarded by the angel. If one were vigilant, one could see the angel moving through the trees at sunset. The truth was, the island was a bit eerie anyway, with no inhabitants. As the boys sat stonelike hoping to catch a glimpse of the spirit, the leaves began to rustle above their heads, and no place else. Branches began to move without even a breath of wind. Paul whispered, "There's no breeze. What's making the trees move?"

Jeed ominously stage whispered, "It's Jehosephat." And even Jeed had to admit he could not explain why the trees continued to move. Paul wasn't kidding. There was no breeze. Josh warbled, "I'm scared," and bolted for the boat. Paul laughed until the trees started swaying again and immediately joined his little brother. From that year on, no vacation at the lake was complete without a night visit to Jehosephat's island, hauling any and all visiting friends along. The annual visit became better than telling ghost stories around the campfire.

Something in Chris rose up as he considered the risks of having Josh initiated. Was Josh the repository of his father's own desires? Was Chris orchestrating this for Josh or for himself? He wanted to be honest with himself. What father does not want a better life for his children? What father does not want his kids to grow up knowing they have been given tools for a rewarding and successful life? Chris's life had been successful without initiation, so why initiation? Life is more than getting; life is also giving, bestowing, blessing, and creating. Yes, that was it. He wanted Josh to know that life was more than busting your ass. Life was to be enjoyed, appreciated, filled with wonder, blessed with growing awareness. "I think the risk is worth it," Chris finally said, staring off into nowhere. "Josh has become aware already that life is more than what a man sees, more than what others tell him to see. I think he will be able to handle initiation. It may scare him, but I think he will move beyond his fear. Besides, he trusts you."

"Then let's do it. Let's put together a ritual." So the rest of the night the two friends discussed ideas and concepts, borrowing from ancient traditions but creating a new and modern way. Both kept wondering about the consequences of what they were messing with. A boy's entire future was at stake.

After concocting the basic agenda of the initiation, Chris summoned his wife and eldest son. Jane wondered what the two of them were up to now. Not often did she see such seriousness on her husband's face. Chris discussed with her and Paul what he planned to do. They, in turn, brought forth their own insights and concerns for Josh. As a mother, Jane had practical concerns about missing a day of school, about food, possible emergencies, and safety. What impact might the ritual have on Josh emotionally and psychologically? Her nervousness was classical, still wanting to protect the boy. She wanted to make sure that Josh was ready for this, and she wanted to be sure that the men did not get him in over his head. But in the end she knew if he were to own his manhood, it would have to be as a man and not as the boy she had nurtured, fostered, and cared for all these years. As she gave her consent and agreed to participate, tears welled up in her hazel eyes. A feeling of compassion filled Jeed as he began to feel the weight of responsibility he was undertaking.

Jane felt the same as Chris regarding a gay man playing such an instrumental role in ushering their sixteen-year-old into manhood. Jane had been quite close to Chris's gay brother, Frank. Being gay was not a loaded topic for her. Frank had been more than the boys' uncle, he had been like a second father. Jane was wisely aware that being gay was far more than a sexual label or cultural phobias.

Despite Chris and Jane's trust, Jeed still felt uneasy about the whole affair. Caring parents had entrusted him with their son, giving up the boy in hopes of getting back a man. Could it be done? What unexpected circumstances, powers, or changes might visit upon this quest? What were they all getting themselves in for?

A date was set. They looked at one another as feelings of excitement and thoughts of anxiety crashed against them. Were they about to awaken an ancient power? Or were they about to fill themselves with dread that would result from their modern frailties? Whether they were ready or not, they were about to find out.

Chapter Six

THE MOTHER BLESSING

W hile getting everything ready in Portland, Jeed began his prayers for Josh's well-being. Though not bodily present, Jeed could feel his spirit watching over Josh. The journey into manhood had begun. He could feel the anxiety and excitement stirring in the air.

Chris and Paul stayed in the background. This was Jane's hour, the hour of the Feminine: the hour of Chaos, Mystery, Wisdom, and Birth. She would have to be the first to let go of the boy, for mothers are blessed with power, fathers with strength. Without power, the man cannot come forward. In certain ancient societies, the mother's letting go involved great drama, even hysteria — railing at the loss of her son, stolen away with great fury and loud noise. Even if the mother felt proud and hopeful in the fact her son was to be initiated as a man, she would make a terrible scene of grief, loss, and breast-beating, to add to the ritual, filling the air with her feminine power — power which could be freely loosed or power which could be traumatically unleashed. Someone had taken her son. Would no one rescue him? Would no one stop the perpetrators — these *men*?

Some mothers prepared themselves for this moment while others did not. Those who did not more than acted out the grieving role. They raged in it, danced a fitful dance of death in it. And woe be it unto the son who had not prepared himself for this moment, either.

In four days Christmas would be celebrated. But already this moment had dulled the power of even Christmas. The frenzy of family shopping no longer occupied everyone's mind. All stopped on this night as one boy, one insignificant boy, took the first step in becoming one wholly and significant man. Jane had already let Josh know she wanted to sit and talk with him this night. This night no phone calls were allowed. His private "teen" line had been disconnected; no one was allowed to come over, and no plans could be made, even through the next day. "Why?" he wanted to know.

"You will find out later," she responded quietly, her eyes meeting his. He had already begun to rebel at this age. How much longer could she get away with unexplained answers? He had been raised with truth, no secrets, honesty, and forthrightness. He was not happy with her keeping a secret from him. Yes, this was the right time to acknowledge his manhood. She could see it in his eyes as he searched hers for answers beyond words.

"Later" had arrived. They sat alone as the lights on the Christmas tree twinkled in merriment. However, no merriment shone on Jane's face. She began her talk with a voice that needed clearing before every sentence.

"Josh, you won't be going to school tomorrow."

"All right!" he grinned back, his braces shining brightly, reflecting the tree lights. Discomfort replaced his cheer as he tried to understand the seriousness occupying her face. With his friends, he often brought levity into serious moments. He was known for his ability to bring cheer, whether at Christmas or any other time. Jane handled Josh's levity with the skills of a diplomat. Not shaming him and not giving in to him, she simply continued the conversation in her matter-of-fact way, speaking with the gentleness of a woman wise with love. She continued, "I've gotten your homework assignments from your teachers. There really isn't much since you're so close to Christmas break. Tonight there are some things you need to do in preparation for tomorrow."

"What is going on, anyway? Dad has been hinting all week that something was going to happen, that I had to keep tomorrow clear. Is anybody going to tell me?"

Jane cleared her throat once again. "Your dad, your brother, and Jeed have been discussing a way of welcoming you into your manhood. I can't tell you any more than to say you will be taken by your brother and your Dad down to the Amtrak station and put on a train to Portland where you will meet Jeed."

"I'm going all by myself?"

"Yes. And there are some things you will need to take with you."

"What's the big secret, anyway? I don't like the idea of all this being a secret. Why can't I be told? What's going to happen? What if I don't want to go down to Portland? It makes me mad that no one is telling me anything!"

Jane had expected this reaction. Typical of her wisdom, she simply responded, "Well, I guess it boils down to whether you trust Jeed or not. You certainly have the right to refuse meeting with him. Do you trust him?"

Josh squirmed at having to make a choice a man would face rather than deferring to what a boy might face by Mom or Dad making the decision for him. Instead of reducing the conversation to a playground response of "Make me!" he had full power to decide whether he would yield to trust and mystery or revolt from decisions made without him, which caused him to feel uneasy and maybe just a bit afraid.

"Course I trust him." Then silence. He began playing with his braces, something he usually did when nervous.

"Well, then, you will need to listen to what else I have to say." He sat in stillness, a bit sullen. The joy of flashing lights and brightly wrapped presents competed with his mood. His eyes slowly traveled up from the floor to meet hers. What had been a grin resigned itself to a straight line.

"OK," he finally agreed.

"You will need to take a knapsack with you, or a book pack, something you can carry. Be sure to take some rain gear with you, an extra pair of thick socks, and a hat or cap. Dress warmly, wear shoes or boots for hiking. Your dad and Paul will give you a few more things in the morning when they take you to the train station. Pack yourself a small lunch to take with you on the train. The lunch is to be eaten only if you feel hypoglycemic; otherwise you are to eat nothing for the rest of the night and tomorrow. You are to fast. I'll wake you in the morning when it's time to go. Any questions?"

A strained pause separated them. Josh felt as if he were about to lose something. He didn't know what. It didn't feel right. A thousand questions wanted to leap out of him, but he knew they would not be answered, perhaps could not be answered. He sat silently, feeling a love for his mother he had never felt before. How strange. What was happening? He watched the tears roll down her cheeks. He wanted to wipe them away, but she beat him to it. Did she feel as if she were about to lose something unexplainable also? Perhaps tomorrow would answer all this.

"No," he answered. "No questions." And that was it. Josh could bounce between extremes like a superball bouncing from floor to ceiling and back. As a youngster, Jeed had nicknamed him "Motor Mouth." On the vacations up to Priest Lake, Jeed had even paid him money to see how long he could keep silent. Laughter always ended the contest. How impossible it was for such an exuberant child to hold his bubbliness. As he grew older, he could swing into long periods of silence in his room , concentrating for hours on the latest adventure game flickering across his computer screen. This night, it seemed, silence would be his companion.

He rose from the couch and strolled into the kitchen. In silence, he proceeded to make a lunch for the following day. Without a word, he retrieved his book pack from the living-room closet, stuffed in the prescribed objects, set all by the front door, and went to bed. That was it. No questions, no antics, no levity.

Jane let out a big sigh, watched the tree lights splash cheerful colors on the ceiling, and thought what tomorrow would bring. She knew that the responsibilities and seriousness of being an adult had always scared Josh. Like some Peter Pan, he had insisted for years he would be a boy forever. The thought that adults even had to pay rent terrified him. How could people make that much money? How would he ever find a way of earning that much money when he grew up? How could a boy find a job that would pay for a car, for clothes, for phone bills? He saw all of this as a kind of threat. The worst kind of threat — death. A death to the joys of boyhood.

Collectively, Jane, Chris, and Jeed had wondered whether Uncle Frank's suicide had somehow fed his Peter Pan complex. Frank's death had devastated the boys. He had been their favorite, their hero — the epitome of the boy-man, the *puer aeternus*. The boys never did see him as "queer," even though he was living with a lover at the time. Frank displayed a completely different outrageousness than did Chris. When Frank spent time up at Priest Lake during summer vacations with the family, he would discuss vivid recurrent dreams and their mystical implications one day, and the next day be out on the shore next to the family trailer, building the most exquisite sandcastle with the boys. The family had a tradition of outdoing all the neighbors on the Fourth of July with fireworks. Frank, being who he was, would turn the giant sandcastle into a launching pad for bottle rockets, firecrackers, and cherry bombs, blowing the hell out of the finely fashioned towers, the driftwood drawbridge, and the sculpted walls. Only Frank could take such hard work and transform it into unbridled fun. Of all Chris's brothers, Frank was Jane's favorite.

Hard rain tapped on the windows in the cold morning darkness of Josh's room as Jane eased open the door. Instead of calling out his name right away, she stood in the flood of light pouring through the door. Josh's outline on the waterbed escaped her at first glance. His slight figure disappeared amongst the embrace of the down comforter and the welcome of the flowing sheets. Temptation tugged at her to let him sleep, to let him remain a boy. After all, he still looked so much like a boy with his short stature, a trait of Chris's side of the family. Unlike the rest of the family, her youngest had stayed skinny his whole life. When had he grown up so quickly?

"Josh?" she called out in a half whisper.

"Uhhh," he gurgled back.

"It's time to get up."

"OK." He didn't move a muscle. Josh tended to wake up with the speed of a blossoming morning glory.

"When you are ready, come downstairs. I have something to say to you before you leave with your dad and brother."

"OK." One eye opened. That was all Jane was looking for. She knew the ritualistic awakening would soon follow. Her rotund figure exited like a shadow fading into the light. The stairs squeaked with every footfall as she tiptoed down the stairs to the living room. Sitting in her typical spot on the couch with her Mickey Mouse blanket draped over her, she waited for Josh to present himself. What would she say? What *should* she say? She had tossed and turned through the night as if her bed had become her enemy. Memories of Josh had danced in and out of her thoughts all night long.

The morning glory had finally crept out of bed. She could hear his closet door squeak open. His next routine would be in front of the mirror, for he was fanatical about his hair. The routine required shampooing, drying, moussing, and making sure every hair stood in place. Oddly enough, he had hated his red hair. She could never forget the day he had come home from school after studying genetics in class. Slinking into the house, he had crashed onto the couch. After several minutes pouting in abject silence, he had finally blurted out, "It's your fault, you know. You're responsible for my birth defect."

"What? What birth defect?" she had asked.

"My red hair! It's a birth defect. And you're responsible," he had said, pouting more seriously.

Jane had erupted into laughter. She couldn't help herself. Josh had always been disturbed about having red hair. He had insisted none of the girls liked him because of it. Which was like claiming mink coats to be ugly because so few people wore them. "It's not a birth defect," she had chortled back. "It's a recessive gene."

"Same difference," he had screeched back. "It's all your fault."

A motherly grin now crept across her face as she thought of him combing his "birth defect" at this moment. Not a hair astray. After a few more minutes, she heard his footsteps on the stairs heading toward the living room. The moment had arrived.

Chris and Paul had already loaded everything in Paul's Gremlin, just waiting for the engine to warm up and Jane to finish the farewell to her youngest's boyhood.

"Where's Dad and Paul?" Josh asked soberly.

"They're waiting out in the car for you. I have a few things to say to you before you leave." He could see his mother's eyes getting red. Whenever her eyes watered like that he grew nervous. For it meant feelings were overflowing with the tears, and he would have to discern the source of the feelings. She was not as easy to read as he. Was she sad or happy? He always wanted to comfort her when she was like this — if she needed comforting. Usually he would try and make a joke to get her to laugh. But no joke could be found.

"Josh, I know how you feel about this trip. You've always been very special to me. When you were still in my womb, it looked like I was going to lose you. I had started bleeding, and the doctors warned me the pregnancy wasn't far enough along for them to be able to do anything. It didn't look good, and they let me know. I remember coming home and telling myself over and over again, 'I'm not going to lose this baby, I'm not going to lose this baby.' I was determined you were going to make it. And you did.

"Many mothers don't like to let go of their children when they grow up. It makes them feel old when their kids grow into adulthood. They like them to stay children as long as they can. They don't want to lose their babies. And I have to confess it is tempting for me to do that with you. But I know it is time for you to accept your manhood. I know this because of the choices I have watched you make and the decisions I have seen you struggle with."

As tears meandered down Jane's freckled cheeks, Josh could only rest his head in his left hand and stare at the carpet. He couldn't watch. He could only listen, his own throat beginning to swell with emotion. Why did she have to put herself through this? This was just one more crazy idea Dad and Jeed had cooked up. It wasn't any big deal, was it? He listened as she cleared her throat a couple of times before continuing.

"You have never liked the idea of having to take on adult responsibility. Yet you didn't hesitate in doing everything in your power to get your driver's license at the earliest possible moment. And now you have it. And I know you understand the adult responsibilities that come with it." Josh became a statue. He couldn't move a muscle. "I want you to know how proud I am of you. I no longer see you as a child but as a man because you have made choices a man would make."

She had observed over the last year how he had treated others, cared for others, spoke his truth even when it wasn't popular. Her faith and trust in him had grown as she saw how his ability to make the right choices along his personal path in life had progressed. He had asked for advice and counsel when he needed guidance, and he had listened to that counsel. When others had needed advice from him, she had watched how he'd taken what he had learned to help and support them. Because of that, she had no trouble in surrendering her own power as a parent to him, because he had earned it. "I have seen how you already are claiming your own power in an unselfish way that does not hurt or demean others, and I give you recognition for that. I want you to know that I respect you and recognize you as a man." Her tears no longer meandered but streamed down her reddening cheeks. She struggled even more for control, her sniffling increasing.

The swelling in his own throat started to ache. *Oh God, I can't cry*, he screamed to himself. *I can't*. He wished this was all over, and at the same time he wished it would never end. Swirling emotions were starting to make him dizzy, his whole body starting to hum. He strained to hold back any betraying tear.

"It's time for you to go with your dad and brother. Remember how proud I am of you and how much I love you." He couldn't say a word. His body had turned to stone. More than anything he wanted to run over and hug her and never let go. But something kept him. The humming grew more pronounced, suddenly broken by the squeaking of the front door. It was Dad.

"Josh, it's time to go. We have to get you to the train."

Stoically, he pulled himself to his feet. Putting on his ski jacket was like trying to put on a straitjacket. All he could do was march to Paul's car like an inmate marching into an insane asylum. He was afraid to say a word for fear of admitting the lump he felt in his throat. Chris looked over at Jane, who had found a kleenex by now. With tenderness, knowing what she must be going through, he walked over to give her a reassuring hug, kissed her wet cheeks and whispered, "Everything will be OK."

A fine misty rain coated everything in wetness as Paul stopped his car in the Amtrak parking lot. The historic depot made the morning darkness seem like a scene out of *Casablanca*. The depot's clock tower showed there wasn't much time left as Chris gathered Josh's things. The two sons were studies in contrast: Paul, sitting smugly with a grin on his face like the cat who ate the canary; Josh, expressionless and as silent as the weeping drizzle. Once inside the station, Chris gathered departure information so Josh could track his way to Portland, and know when to get off. The three sat on one of the old wooden benches lining the interior of the large depot. With each passing minute, Josh's face grew more troubled. The echoes of the depot reminded him of a tomb.

"Dad, I don't think I want to go through with this."

Chris leaned forward to gather his thoughts. He had tried to prepare himself for this. "Why, what's the matter?"

"All this secrecy. It bothers me. I don't like not knowing what's going on. It makes me feel bad inside. I don't feel right. Maybe we can do this another time."

Chris's first temptation was to give his youngest son a good ribbing. After all, the acorn doesn't fall very far from the tree. It's what Josh would do if the roles were reversed. But he felt the anxiety that had been hanging in the air the whole drive down to the station. Secrecy was a new experience for this family. "Josh, I know we never keep secrets in our family. We've always been able to share things as a family, able to talk about anything and everything. There is a reason why this is different. I know it's hard for you to understand. But hang in there. I ask you to trust me on this. It will be worth it."

There was that word again: "trust." How could he object or argue about such a word, which was so close to words like "love" and "devotion" and "honesty"? Why was such a word causing him so much anxiety? He felt mixed up inside. His mom's words still stirred within him. What was this conspiracy he could not know about? He felt so alone. How was it possible for these people who loved him so much, who now conspired in secrecy, to dare ask for his trust? He felt like screaming with frustration.

"All right, Dad. But I don't like it."

"I understand, Son. Just hang in there."

Josh gasped, running his fingers through his flawless hair. "OK. OK. Let's get on with it."

Paul sat through the whole incident in total silence, still wearing his Cheshire cat grin. Chris smiled warmly at his son's triumph, his passing of the first test. "There are a few things I need to say to you, first. Here is a letter from Jeed. You are to read it only after the train has left the station." He handed Josh a business-size envelope with his name neatly printed on the outside. Next he handed Josh a notebook of rather fine quality with two pens carefully chosen by Mom and Dad. The notebook bore intricate, beautiful Native American designs. All the pages inside were blank, empty. Empty was how Josh felt at this moment. About to be abandoned. "This journal is for you to write everything down about your experience. The letter will tell more. Please keep in mind you aren't to talk to anyone during the whole trip unless it is necessary. If you need help, don't hesitate to ask the conductor. He will be the guy in a blue uniform. Otherwise, stay in your thoughts as you get ready to meet Jeed in Portland. He will be waiting for you at the train station down there."

Chris continued, "Remember that the intent is to also continue your fast. If you feel like you need to eat because of low blood sugar, then by all means, eat your lunch. You can throw away what you don't use when you reach Portland. Do you have any questions?"

"No" was all that he said. Chris handed Josh his ticket. With a growing seriousness on his face, Josh jerked the ticket from his father's hand. Without a hug or a word good-bye, he gathered his belongings and trudged out to the boarding ramp, climbed aboard the train, and disappeared. Like one of the carvings on Easter Island he sat there and stared into emptiness, unable to bear looking out the window. If he saw his dad, he was afraid he'd jump off the train and into his arms.

Chris and Paul watched until the train crawled out of sight. Both felt a kind of excitement well within them. The quest had begun.

As the train pulled out of the yard, Josh pulled the envelope out of his pocket and ripped it open. Two pages of neatly printed writing stared back at him, followed by two blank pages. He hoped the letter would relieve some of the mystery and abandonment that filled him.

Dear Josh,

As you read this, you are on the train coming down to meet me. I will be at the train station as you arrive. From there, you and I will then travel to a special spot where we will discuss why this journey has been arranged for you.

You have reached the age of manhood, and it is important that we older men in your life welcome you into your manhood. I know manhood is not something you have looked forward to. I know you would like to stay a boy. But life sometimes will not wait on us.

Sometimes we have to take on things even when we think we are not ready. You have just received your driver's license and have stepped into the world of adults by stepping on the gas pedal of a car that only you control. Whether you are ready or not, you have already made the decision to accept responsibility. Your driver's license is a symbol of the power you hold in our modern world: the power to be independent, the power to explore on your own, the power to assist others no matter how far away, and even the power to kill, whether recklessly or by accident. And the only way to honor this power, this responsibility, is to welcome you into the world of men.

As an Elder, it is my duty to bring the forces together which will help you in your journey as a man. You are taking your first step into manhood by taking this train trip all by yourself. Sometimes a man must do things alone. Sometimes a man must do things when everyone around him says not to. Sometimes a man must live by his own convictions, and try to change the wrongs around him when no one else will help. It is the responsibility of an Elder to help you learn how to do this. Today is the first stage in bringing you tools that will serve you well on your journey into manhood.

As you take this trip down to meet me, there are certain things I would like you to think about on your trip. For I will ask you to give your answers to these questions:

1. Are you prepared to begin to understand your own gifts that you were born with to make this world a better place? For a man to help others, he must first understand himself. The time is now for you to recognize the gifts you have inherited, understand them, and use them wisely.

2. Do you understand that a man must honor himself by being true to who he is? That means when you accept responsibilities, you carry them out to the best of your ability. That means you live in integrity by not being false to yourself and thereby not being false to others. That means you must learn to walk in the spirit world as

well as in this world. Every man needs the help of the spirits and the angels in his journey through life. When your mother or father can't be with you, there will be times when you will need help from the Otherworld. As you grow older, I will teach you more about this Otherworld.

3. What part of yourself do you not like? What are the parts of yourself that you fear? Write in your journal the answers to these questions. Every man must face his own Shadow, his own shortcomings, his own terror of who he is or is not. This means you must eventually face the parts of yourself you feel are weak or inadequate or capable of failure. Once you face them, you then are *not* controlled by them. But you will need the help of other men, trusted men, to face your Shadow. This is something that may take years. But I want you to take the first step in facing your Shadow as you come to meet me.

4. What part or parts of yourself do you most admire? Write in your journal your answer. So many men walk the Earth with no love for themselves or no appreciation for who they are. If we allow this to happen, these men become zombies, the walking dead. Our world is full of them. I have watched how, as a boy, you have oftentimes criticized yourself for not being good enough. Now it is time for you to tell me how and why you are good enough to enter your manhood.

5. I would like you to write a story or a poem or draw a picture of Joshua who is the boy, and then do the same thing of Josh who is the man. I will ask you to do something with this later. I have included two extra pieces of paper in case you didn't bring your journal. If you don't have a pencil or pen, ask the conductor if you might borrow one. If he or she doesn't have one or can't get you one, then ask where you might be able to acquire one.

6. And finally, I wish to talk to you about your power animal and your angel as you are on this journey. As you take the train down to me, I want you to be very silent and find out if you hear a voice

91

inside you that says things to you. I want you to keep trying to hear this voice during the whole trip. If you don't hear this voice, that's OK. But if you do, please write down everything you hear within you.

You are a very special human being who has come into this world as a boy. It is now time for you to begin to understand and begin to use these special gifts that make you Josh-the-man. The older men in your life will help you with this. As you grow, we will grow with you. There will be things you will teach us as we teach you. And as fellow men, we will call each other brothers, knowing we have much to bring to one another to make this world a better place for all to grow and live in love.

See you soon,
Jeed

Chapter Seven

BOY AND MAN

*T*he mantra of the wheels clacking against the tracks gently began to calm Josh with its heartbeat sound. Like an ancient rhythm that has existed since the beginning of humanity, the womblike thump-thump tolled out the voice of life itself: all is well, all is well. As it wove a spell over him, he stared out the window transfixed by the blur of passing naked trees, the dance of nature in scene after passing scene of forest, sea, and clouds. The rocking of the train felt like the arms of a mother comforting her newborn, welcoming him into a harsh world.

"Tickets, please," the conductor sang out. Josh watched the conductor's reflection in the window. The man was staring at him. What was he supposed to do? Anxiety flooded him as the towering man in uniform stood his ground like some figure from *Star Wars*. Where was his ticket? Oh yeah, Dad had put it in his shirt pocket. The conductor smiled reassuringly, seeing the worried look on the young man's face. "Your first trip?" he asked knowingly. Josh nodded his head yes, making sure to keep his vow of silence. "Going to Portland, I see. We should be there in about four more hours. I'll let you know when we get close." Josh sat stoically, not wanting to be rude but also not wanting to betray his taciturnity. "If you have any questions or you need anything, you can ask me or the steward who will be in charge of this car. You'll be seeing her in a little bit." Once again nodding, he smiled with appreciation. "Have a nice trip." The conductor continued his song in tune with the mantra of the heartbeat sound, "Tickets, please."

Jeed's letter still clung to his hands. His reading it had changed everything. The journey now seemed less a mystery and more of an adventure. *What is going to happen to me? Where is Jeed going to take me?* The questions would not stop stampeding through his brain. *Is he going to leave me alone in some isolated place?* He had studied at school how some Native American boys entered into manhood. And most terrifying of all, *What if I have to take all my clothes off? What if I have to be naked in some kind of ceremony?* Josh's intellect proved his own worst enemy at times. Sometimes, he simply knew too much, thought too much. His imagination could provoke incredible dramas.

As an eight-year-old boy, Paul could drive horror into him by simply teasing, "I can see your underwear!"

"No you can't," he'd scream back.

"Yes I can, yes I can! There it is, it's white with a red stripe on top. I can see your underwear," he'd sing. Paul could be a merciless tease at times.

"Mom!" he'd cry out, knowing no other course. And then the inevitable scream of pain — tears by the bucketful. Jane would come running, thinking for sure Josh had broken an arm or leg by the sound of the window-rattling scream. "Mom," he sobbed uncontrollably, "Paul can see my underwear." It would take all her composure not to burst out laughing. But at the same time, a lesson needed to be learned.

"Paul, why do you tease him so?" she would ask in a nice way so as not to fill her older son with needless guilt.

"What's the big deal about underwear, anyway?" he wanted to know. Paul was already a student of magic, able to manage complex feats with slight-of-hand in front of his classmates. But this was the best magic of all. He could transform his younger brother into a blithering ball of uncontrollable sobbing with a single sentence.

"Josh," Jane cooed, "Paul is just teasing you. Don't worry, no one can really see your underwear." She knew Paul had seen the clothes laid out earlier.

"Are you sure?" Her comforting arms quieted him quickly.

"Yes. The only way I can see your underwear is if I pull your shirt out." That seemed to work, except the next time she knew Paul, in all his cleverness, would pull the shirt out to create the desired effect. "You should try not to believe everything you hear. Try not to be so sensitive to the teasing of others. It's not that terrible if someone sees your underwear."

On more than one occasion, Jeed had witnessed this underwear magic act. After a full year of watching Paul repeat this power over his brother, Jeed realized Josh didn't really have this inordinate phobia of having his underwear spotted. Even Jeed had tried this scene out once when he actually *could* spy Josh's underwear. What was really the cause of the trouble was the lad's own tender heart. The fact that someone would want to make him cry, made him cry. Why would someone want to hurt him? What horrible acts had he committed to warrant such treatment? What was a mother to do with two sons of such contrasting archetypal power? One a Magician, the other a Lover.

Josh stared at the envelope in his hand, wondering whether it contained treasure or curse. He slowly unfolded the pages again. A strange feeling moved through him as if he had immersed himself in weightless outer space. Was it the letter? Was it the train? Was it the fact that he hadn't eaten anything for breakfast? The words in the letter asked him to listen within, to try and hear an inner voice. Was this weird feeling that voice trying to talk to him, making him feel so disoriented? Teetering between wishing he could get off the train or giving in to the strange feeling, he took a deep breath and tried to listen. He could hear his own heart thumping in rhythm with the clackity-clack of the train. His whole body began to tingle, but he could hear nothing. No voice. *Maybe I'm not doing it right*, he thought. *Maybe I am supposed to do something else.* He decided to read the letter a third time.

When Jeed had written the letter, it had been his intent to introduce Josh to new thoughts, new worlds, and even new realities. What would happen beyond the introduction was up to Josh. There was so much for the lad to think about, but one thing was plain. He may have thought this whole idea was crazy to begin with, but no longer. Now it excited him, scared him, made him feel alive like he never had before. Now it was real. He could feel his fear of being alone on this fast-moving train, fear of ending up God-knows-where with Jeed — or without Jeed. The mystery of what might befall him created a tightness in his gut, which wouldn't go away. Maybe he really was a man. Maybe there *was* something here trying to connect with him, something he couldn't put his finger on. The emotions washing through him were yielding to a sense of inevitability of confronting his own adult self, confronting a growing sense of commitment, filling his lungs and his bowels with a kind of newfound courage, strength. He *would* confront the unknown and deal with it.

With bravado, he unzipped his book bag and pulled out the sack lunch as if it were an emergency parachute. Furtively, he peered down the train aisle, past all the rows of seats filled with holiday travelers, and spotted his goal. With purpose in his step, he tramped to the middle of the car where the stairwell descended to the lower level. A stainless steel water fountain hid, recessed into the wall. Next to the fountain huddled a trash bin. With a sturdy toss he threw the sack lunch into the receptacle, tramped back to his seat and sat in a kind of steeled silence. Josh had on his game face. Only this time, the game was not baseball, it was life.

After staring out the window at a passing town, he searched the book bag again and pulled out the journal his dad had given him. Taking one of the pens from his pocket, he began to write.

I'm not sure I know the difference between Josh, the boy, and Josh, the man. I see the boy who is selfish, thinking only of himself. He complains a lot and wants a lot of things from Mom and Dad. He likes to pick on his older brother.

Interesting how Josh's relationship with Paul had progressed over the years. While in their grade-school years, they showed no mercy to one another. In exchange for Paul's being a merciless tease, Josh had grown into Paul's alter-ego, it seemed. Like Kato attacking Clouseau in *The Pink Panther*, Josh would jump into his favorite Bruce Lee imitation at a moment's notice if Paul appeared the least bit vulnerable. The two were a comedy act unsurpassed even by Peter Sellers. Anyone witnessing their make-believe kung fu fights hopelessly fell into laughter ... except Paul. Paul knew what was coming — an attack on the back or a karate chop to the head.

Paul was no small kid. His weight was enough to qualify him for the Refrigerator Perry football award. He rarely used his bulk to punish his younger brother for pouncing on him, or pounding on him. But Josh's intent was not so thoughtful. If Paul managed to headlock the pint-size Bruce Lee or otherwise immobilize him, Josh would inevitably counter with a whack to Paul's crotch. And Paul would inevitably crash to the floor, screaming bloody murder, fake or otherwise. It made the casual onlooker wince. How Paul made it past puberty with the family jewels intact was beyond anyone.

Josh continued to scribble in his journal:

Josh, the boy, is a good athlete and is popular at school. He likes to make his friends laugh. But he's unsure of himself. He hates to lose and gets mad if he doesn't win.

It was true. Josh had natural athletic abilities, in spite of his shortness. And he did hate to lose at almost anything, especially in junior high school. As he wrote the words, he smiled as he remembered the night the whole family, along with Jeed, had gone to the movie *Revenge of the Nerds*. The popular movie made it cool to be nerdy. During the ride back, Chris described his own high-school days when he suffered greatly for being one of the nerdy types, having been poked fun at on a regular basis. Jeed chimed in with a similar story of how he had been near the top of the nerd pile, not even able to find a date for the junior prom except with a girl who was considered queen of the nerdettes. Paul echoed how he felt he was a kind of nerd at school in spite of being popular. He then asked, "Mom, were you a nerd?" After some time she confessed that, yeah, she guessed she had been kind of a nerd herself.

Of course, following this exposé, Josh insisted in a whiny voice, "Well, I'm a nerd, too."

Paul choked on his laughter. "No, you're not. You're a jock."

"No, I'm not! I'm a nerd!"

"No, Josh," Jeed added. "You lettered in sports, and you're popular with the girls. You're a jock."

"Yeah," Chris agreed humorously as he peered at his youngest in his rearview mirror.

The nodding heads craned to see the source of the soft weeping, which grew into a full bawl. "I don't want to be a jock. I want to be a nerd like the rest of the family." Tears in full flush. Everyone broke into laughter. Everyone except Josh — the jock. Another Joshism had been created. The story would be told repeatedly over the years how Mom had to come to the rescue once again to let him know it was OK to be a jock.

Josh could still hear the laughter in his head as he tried to think more of what to write about Josh-the-boy. *This isn't easy*, he thought to himself. He'd never paid much attention to being a boy. He just was. Not something you think about. The only time he'd ever really thought about who he was occurred when Mom and Dad had taken the two boys to a family therapist at Group Health. Chris and Jane had heard the boys making certain self-condemning comments, which caused them concern as parents. They wondered if the boys were adapting well to everyday society. The therapist had given both sons an assignment. They had to look into a mirror each morning and say three positive things to the boy in the mirror. Josh remembered how he had stood in front of the mirror for quite a long time, unable to think of even one good thing to say about himself. He had started to feel embarrassed. Not until Jane peeked in to see how he was doing did he give up, breaking into a rosy blush.

"Mom, I can't think of anything to say," he confessed. She tried to give him some pointers on how to find at least one good thing to say about himself in the mirror, but she didn't want to do it for him. For another fifteen minutes he struggled, before a lightbulb went on in his head. He grinned with embarrassment and said in his most sheepish manner, "You have nice hair." He had giggled when he said it, for he really felt dumb. Now, having to write down words in this blank journal seemed equally dumb. But he struggled on.

> As a boy, I like to have fun. So I don't always clean my room when I should. I don't always do the dishes when I should. And I don't always take out the trash when it's my turn. I love to play baseball and throw the ball against the garage door in the back yard.

> As a boy, I am sometimes afraid I might get beaten up at school. Sometimes I'm afraid guys who are in gangs are going to cause trouble and knife me or something. And I'm afraid to die.

For reasons he didn't understand, the last sentence he wrote was the last sentence that needed to be written about the boy. There was no more to say. It left him with a chill. Pulling his jacket up around his neck, he stared out the train window once again, noticing how the terrain had changed greatly. The serene beauty of Puget Sound had replaced the blur of buildings. On the horizon, the choppy waters melted into the sky with matching grayness. Clam diggers could be seen here and there, searching for booty. His thoughts now drifted to the next topic he was to write about. Who was Josh, the man?

Josh was not the only one steeped in deep thought. Down in Portland, Jeed, too, was wading through questions that challenged his role as an Elder while his charge sped toward him on steel rails. Jeed had intended to spend the day praying for Josh as the soon-to-be initiate journeyed south, but now he found his prayers directed more at himself. Was he worthy as a man to lead this lad into his manhood? If the previous attempt with Paul had failed, what made him think this attempt would not fail also?

The time grew near when Jeed would have to leave for the train station. *If only I could notify Amtrak and have them send the Coast Starlight back to Seattle,* he fretted. As nervous energy began to crawl up the back of his neck, Jeed became aware of how he had switched the focus from Josh to himself. *Of course I'm not worthy to take on the role of Elder,* he decided. *Who is?* The truth is that such matters are never successfully carried out by one man. Without the spirit realm, this would be little more than an exercise in ego. *I have to stop dwelling on myself,* he thought. If he were to be instrumental in initiating Josh, he would have to forget about himself, his weaknesses, his shortcomings. Instead, he needed to concentrate on gathering the forces of the ancestors, the angelic forces that open the heavens, as well as those who shepherd the Earth. He knew that such a communion was required to make our own foibles and imperfections irrelevant, non-interfering. Our true humanity rests not in the territoriality of the two square feet of space we occupy upon the Earth. We are more fully human if our connectedness to the infinite can couple with being anchored in the finite. He had learned this from Malidoma. So he continued in his praying, this time not only for Josh but also for himself and the efforts the two were about to engage. A sixteen-year-old boy was headed his way, and Jeed knew that he had to find a place within himself where the two could be pulled into the infinite.

As Josh stared at a new blank page in his journal, he pondered who at school he considered to be a man, someone his own age.

Combing his thoughts, he tried hard to conjure up a candidate. He thought of some of the tough guys who ran with the gangs. They tried to act like men but they were really all about show. He could tell they neither cared about themselves nor anyone else — just looking good, macho. All they did was cause trouble. They were nothing but echoes from *Lord of the Flies*. They couldn't begin to display what was was good in themselves, the school, or society in general. They only stood for acting strong in order to hide their deep fears of being weak. No, they weren't men; they were simply boys trying to play at being men. Nobody at school was fooled. So who was a man? He could think of no one his own age whom he would consider to be a man. He even had difficulty thinking of teachers he would consider to be men. Perhaps only one: Mr. Yudein.

Mr. Yudein lived peacefully within himself. He went to great lengths to try and instill a sense of self-trust, self-esteem, and self-confidence in his students as part of learning in the classroom. There was no one like him. Many of his fellow teachers acted like little more than petty lords over fiefdoms — intellectual bullies. To them, students represented little more than objects to further their professional goals, or enemies to be conquered, or empty bowls into which they alone could pour their hallowed knowledge. And woe be it unto any student who would not show proper respect to these hallowed ones. No, these were not men; they were nothing more than boys in men's bodies.

So what was it to be a man? As he picked up his pen, he decided to write whatever came into his mind. Perhaps thinking about such matters only made them more difficult to figure out.

Josh the Man.

Being young, I realize things will probably still change for me. But I will explore what has happened up to now. I notice, right off, the fact that my confidence is a lot better than before high school. I have opened my eyes and am starting to see things in a whole new way. I have learned that girls are not to be feared but enjoyed, a balance of mutual love and respect.

Over time, I have mellowed out and become less aggressive. I accept my looks and like them a lot better. The biggest thing I am working on is being more understanding of my friends. I have noticed at times that I can be a real jerk to them.

Life seems to be at a peak right now. I hope in the years to come I can remain like this and help others achieve this.

One last thing I noticed is that I am STARVING! Now I have a better understanding of how bad Somalia was.

As hard as he tried, there was little more he could write. He didn't know what else to say. When he thought about "growing up," he knew it felt scary. But when he tried to put it down on paper, he didn't know exactly what the scariness was about. In fact, he didn't know how words could say what manhood was. He knew what it wasn't. And there the mystery began to unfold.

With a sense of frustration, he closed his journal. Why did he let himself get talked into this? None of it made a lick of sense. Welling feelings of anger mixed with the frustration. He remembered from old movies how one could pull a cord, and the train would come to a screeching halt. If only there were a cord, he'd pull it right now. Voices that couldn't be heard, topics he couldn't write about, memories that only haunted him — all reminded him of how insecure he felt as to what it meant to be a man.

With finality, he set his journal down, put his book pack against the window, and lay his head on it. Pushing the seat button, he reclined and watched the world go by. Like a serpent seeking prey, the train crawled through the bare trees lining the track. Josh felt as if he had been swallowed whole, trapped in its belly. The passing Douglas firs stood calmly as if silently spying on him, guarding some mystery pulling him toward Portland. What was going to happen to him? Back and forth the rail car swayed, as if trying to comfort him

amid so much unknown, so much aloneness. He could have been at
school with his friends right now. Maybe even having a Christmas
party in one of the rooms. But no, here he sat in the belly of a
mechanical beast, its metal body carrying him farther and farther
away from the life he had known. His head started to nod. Voices. He
could hear voices. Were these the voices that Jeed had written about?
The train sounds muffled; the world began to fade. The voices called
to him. Did they say he was about to die?

Chapter Eight

THE KEY OF SILENCE

*P*Portland in thirty minutes," yelled the conductor, waking Josh from his dream. The approach to Portland filled Josh with anxiety, made only worse by the dream. What did the dream mean? Jeed had taught him that some Native American traditions believed dreams to be the real world, while waking reality came from a make-believe world. Native Americans spent serious time and effort exploring powerful dreams like the one from which he had just awakened. He could only remember standing naked before an old man dressed in animal skins, who had asked him questions for which he had no answers. The sense of failure plagued him as he awoke from the barking of the conductor.

As the train crawled to a halt, Jeed felt joy and excitement vibrating within him. He had looked forward to seeing Josh. His godson was always a delight, one way or the other. Craning his neck, trying to spy the lad amidst the crowd of holiday travelers, Jeed began to wonder if Josh had backed out. But Chris surely would have called. Finally, he spotted the red hair of a rather disgruntled hobbit in the back of the pack. His short stature made it difficult for Jeed to read his face with so many arrivals bobbing around him. Not until his charge drew close did Jeed notice the boy's stone face and locked jaw. *Probably a product of the mystery and self-examination,* Jeed thought. Josh snapped to a stop in front his self-proclaimed Elder. No hug, no hi, no nothing. Just a hangdog head staring at the ground with resignation.

"Hey, Josh," Jeed chortled in normal fashion.

"Hi" was all he managed in a half-hearted tone.

"How was the trip?"

"Long." He had his game face on. Jeed couldn't tell if he was pissed or just serious.

"If you have to go to the bathroom, now's a good time to go, 'cause we won't be stopping anyplace where a restroom will be available."

"No. Let's get on with this," he breathed out as he shifted from one foot to the other.

"OK. From here on out, I'm going to ask you to continue in silence. I will be maintaining silence myself. If you feel there is something you need to say, then say it only if it's important." How far they had come since the early years when Jeed had paid quarters to the little Motor Mouth for silence. "You won't be knowing where we are going until we get there. If you have any other bags to pick up here at the depot, now is the time to get them."

"No. Let's go," he spoke quietly, almost with relief. The two headed out of the depot, and crossed the Old Town cobblestone street where Jeed's jeep waited. Opening the rear door, Jeed loaded Josh's pack next to his own. Pangs of uncertainty swept through Jeed as he buckled himself into the driver's seat. His thoughts drifted back to the day Malidoma had given the men's group studying with him an exercise. They were to find the Key of Silence. All were to enter the woods of the Oregon Coast Range in solitude with nothing but the clothes on their backs. A nearby vacation house belonged to one of the men participating in the weekend intensive with Malidoma. The objective was to enter fully into Nature alone, find a place where each could spend time in silence until he could communicate with a tree spirit or nature spirit. If no spirit appeared, then meditation was the alternative.

Jeed remembered how he had climbed high on one of the mountains, and found a small brook trickling around an old-growth fir. A severe windstorm had toppled many trees weeks before, but this big guy had stood strong as if a king at court with his tree subjects bowed down before him. Sadness came over Jeed at witnessing so many beautiful trees prostrate like dead soldiers from a killer wind, knowing that the inevitable forest fires would soon follow, turning the once magnificent trees to ash. He heard someone laughing and immediately spun around searching for the source. Was someone following him? Altering his concentration, he used his "other" eyes to search the area, as Malidoma had taught him, and spied a small elfin spirit next to the grandfather tree. Malidoma had spoken of such beings. This was how the *Kontomblé* sometimes appeared. No sooner had his mind thought the word "Kontomblé" than the critter jumped into the brook and disappeared. The *Kontomblé* are considered the highest form of nature spirit by the Dagara. *A sign*, Jeed thought. *This is where I am to meditate for the day.* He sat for hours listening to the breath of the wind, the voice of the stones in the brook, watching birds circle overhead or dash through the remnant of forest, returning his focus to the brook, hoping the *Kontomblé* would reappear. A chill swept down from the mountain as the clouds grew thick overhead. Snow? It was then he heard the tree.

Why do you sit before me? he heard in his mind. Had he found the Key of Silence? Was he making this up? Was the tree truly speaking to him in the silence? He decided to answer back in silence.

I have come to listen, to learn. My friend Malidoma says you carry much wisdom, not unlike the River People. Malidoma had spoken of the large smooth stones at the bottom of rivers as the River People. These the Dagara considered the most wise of spirits.

Why do you wear clothing? For your friend also taught you how to bring energy from the air, the ancient tree said. Jeed thought about it a minute.

107

It's freezing cold out here, he objected. *But what the hell? If I'm here to learn, I'm here to learn.* Reluctantly, he stood up, looked around, and, seeing no one, stripped naked, piling his clothes next to the brook. He tried to sit on the brush-covered ground. The fir needles and twigs poking against his privates and anus proved too much distraction. Wiping his bottom clean, he pulled his jacket under him and returned to his meditating position. The cold bit against his skin. Slowly, he focused more and more on his solar plexus, visualizing the sun within him. With love in his heart, he invited heat from the earth and comfort from the wind to surround him. Magically, the cold disappeared, leaving him quite comfortable even as snowflakes began to fall. *Breathtaking*, he thought, *absolutely breathtaking.* Closing his eyes, he began to hear the tree humming a song. He could not make out the words, for they sounded like some foreign tongue. Then he began to hear a similar song within himself. Where did it come from? The tree stopped its song, leaving only the song within Jeed growing louder and louder.

This is the song of your soul, said the grandfather fir. *This is the song that allows you into the Otherworld. You will take many there.*

What? Jeed thought. *How can that be?* The group of men at this outing had committed to studying with Malidoma for a full year, with the end result being that of having a chance to enter the Otherworld, a Dagara word for worlds beyond ordinary reality, with him. The previous year another group of men had studied with him for a year in hopes of entering the Otherworld. But when the moment came, and the threshold opened, they bailed out, not being able to handle the energy or the wildness of the experience. Malidoma had made it plain to this current group of men that the journey would not be easy. What did the tree mean that Jeed, himself, would lead others across this threshold to the Otherworld? The question jarred Jeed out of his meditation. There he sat, naked as a lawn ornament, realizing the night was setting in on him. As he turned to find his watch, he froze in disbelief. Before him stretched hundreds and hundreds of spider webs. Some were intact while others hung as strands gently swaying with the quiet breeze. Thousands of snowflakes had attached themselves to the spider webs, tiny white Christmas garlands hanging from the many branches surrounding Jeed. About half an inch of snow had accumulated on the ground. Had he been that deep in mediation so as not to notice? He grabbed his watch. "Holy shit," he whispered. He was two hours past the time all the men were to return to the retreat house. They surely must have sent out a search party by now. Grabbing his clothes, he began to dress himself, still spellbound by the stunning beauty of the hundreds of spider webs dressed in snowflake garlands. How had he not noticed these webs earlier? Had they been there when he first arrived? He didn't remember any brushing against his face. Was this the work of the *Kontomblé*? Was this a sign of affirmation to celebrate the message of the grandfather tree? *Craziness. All of this borders on craziness*, Jeed thought as he fumbled to don his shoes. Not until he zipped up his coat did he once again feel the cold against him. "None of this makes sense," he mumbled. "I'm losing it."

After rushing down the mountainside, he arrived at the house with night fully fallen. Lights shone all around the vacation home. One of the men had opened the back door to dump the garbage when Jeed walked up. "There you are," he said. "Malidoma said you'd be showing up soon. Have a good time?"

Jeed let out a sigh of relief. Thank God a search party hadn't been sent out. "Incredible," he answered. "Simply incredible." The next day, after one of the group exercises, Jeed decided to tell Malidoma about the previous night and what the grandfather fir had said. The African only grunted in response. And that was it.

When the year of study was up, Malidoma once again opened the threshold to the Otherworld. And like the previous group of men, this group also pulled back from the experience. Except one. Only one stepped through the threshold. Would Josh be the first he would try to show the Otherworld to? Could he? Should he? Jeed shivered as he turned the ignition key. What were the spirits asking of him?

The high rev of the Samurai engine drowned out all thought as they turned onto Broadway, crossing the old bridge over the Willamette River. As they merged onto Interstate 5, Jeed began to ponder the carefully laid plans made around the initiation and whether they would provoke their desired effect. He and Josh were two men propelling themselves into a realm where neither had ever been. Sure, Jeed had participated in rituals before, but none that lasted all day long or involved the initiation of a young man. Jeed's involvement in church liturgy, both on a local level and a national level, had prepared him for the power and the spiritual interaction required in ritual. But at the same time, the true essence, the true power of ritual rests in letting go, opening ourselves to the incoming and the assistance of other beings, other realities. Ritual requires a humility that liturgy does not. To Jeed, liturgy oftentimes seemed more an enactment of ego than an act of worship. Mystery necessarily stood at the heart of ritual. Consequently, with Jeed's knowing this, a nervous energy permeated the cab of the Suzuki Samurai. The truth be told, neither Jeed nor Josh knew what was about to happen.

As they crossed the Columbia River into Vancouver, Washington, more and more uncertainty filled the air. Turning east onto Highway 14, the two travelers headed toward the Columbia River Gorge from the Washington side. On the opposite side of the river, Interstate 84 stood like a monument to modern technology. Oregon and Washington had fought hard for the interstate to be on its side of the river. Oregon won out. And unlike Oregon's, the Washington side remained undeveloped and simple. With one noted exception. The James River pulp mill dominated the upcoming town of Camas. With his nose wrinkled, Josh wondered if Jeed had cut the cheese. In spite of the wonders to be found on the Washington side of the Columbia River, the pulp mill stood as an ominous reminder of the influence of man over nature. As Jeed peered at Josh, he could tell that the lad was wondering if he should roll down the window. Jeed decided to say nothing about how the smell would only grow worse with the window down.

As the Suzuki rumbled past the ugly sludge ponds, Jeed decided to slow down a bit, for he wished Josh to experience the full impact of this man-made wonder. On the right side of the highway, huge fountains sprayed into the air what looked like liquid shit. In a way, these fountains represented man's testimonial in trying to unpollute the very water that man had intentionally polluted, not realizing that in turn the air itself would become polluted. The life-filled waters of the Columbia waterway lay only a few hundred yards away, betrayed by its sister river, the Washougal, prostituted into service to carry the effluent of the pulp plant into the Columbia ecosystem. The pulp mill itself stunned the eyes. So large was its footprint on shore that few could tell which was larger, the monstrous plant or the town of Camas. Fumaroles from steel pipes snorted into the air in such quantities that the structure appeared as some surreal dragon raging against any who dared enter the Gorge. Even the plant's metal exterior resembled dragon scales painted a strange green, adding to the eerie presence. Josh couldn't take the smell any longer and cranked down his window. In a few seconds he discovered his mistake. Staying silent proved a difficult task. All he could do was stare at Jeed as if to say, *What in hell have you taken me to?* Rolling the window back up served little purpose. Josh held his breath as if desperately trying to escape a gas attack. In a moment of compassion, Jeed decided to push the jeep past the speed limit, and headed for their true destination, some twenty more miles up the Columbia Gorge.

The deeper they journeyed into the sacred confines of the Columbia River, the more austere and majestic nature arrayed itself. Tremendous cliffs jutted up on either side of the river, remnants of an ice age that had created a gigantic dam of ice, in what is now Idaho, which eventually burst to release the largest flood ever to hit the planet. The horrendous volumes of water carved walls through the Cascade Mountains like a miniature Grand Canyon, creating what today is the giant half tube that is called the Gorge. At each end of this horseshoe-shaped channel, extremes in climate rage warnings to any and all who enter the private domain of the gods. The east side can either throw extremely high or low temperatures at any who dare enter. Though deceptively verdant and lush, great winds or torrential rains constantly rack the west side. No wonder that the Gorge reigns as the windsurfing capital of the world.

111

The sense of isolation wore on Josh as the two men traveled farther and farther away from civilization. *Where are we going?* he wondered. Anxiety made his lips disappear into his mouth, leaving only a shortened line on his smooth young face. As they wandered farther into the Gorge, Jeed wanted to ask Josh how he was doing. The lad still possessed those boyish moments when one couldn't tell what strange notion might dance forth from his fertile mind. But no, silence had to weave its magic. *A man needs to learn to stay in his thoughts, work things out for himself*, Jeed reminded himself. The Key of Silence had to be found.

With the stench of the pulp mill finally dissipating as they entered the Gorge, a brisk wind, fresh and clean from the distant desert, filled the cab with the scent of sage. What a contrast from the pulp mill. Colors heightened in the absence of smog, and evergreens waved as if trying to catch the eye. The whitecaps on the Columbia foamed into a rich white frosting on a green and blue glaze. A change in weather approached. *Looks like we'll be hiking in the rain after all*, Jeed thought. Would it dampen the effect of the rituals? What was it about ritual that the Dagara believed essential to everyday life? Working with Malidoma had broadened Jeed's awareness regarding the power associated with inviting spirit beings into significant moments of one's life. It was one thing to attend church on Sundays and pray to God, praise God, thank God, and say good-bye to God, followed by six days given to little thought of honoring God. It was quite another matter to invite in spirit beings to assist with the everyday happenings in life, no matter what day of the week.

Jeed had been taught to say grace before meals. Though a nice gesture, the blessing had held as much power as folding his underwear because it had become little more than rote, a habit. All of that changed after his reading Dorothy Maclean's book *To Hear the Angels Sing*. He began to honor all of life in much the same way that Saint Francis of Assisi had. Well known for prayers aimed at Brother Sun or Sister Moon, Francis had frequently conversed with Brother Spider and Sister Sparrow. Jeed could still remember the first time he seriously looked at a piece of broccoli and thanked the angels responsible for its flourishing. No longer was it a mere vegetable. It had become an acknowledged part of life, his life, the circle of life.

Friends began to look at Jeed strangely when they accompanied him on a group Christmas tree hunt. After finding the perfect tree for himself and Nattie, he laid hands on the tree and asked its permission to take it home, then gave thanks for its giving up of its life. Jokes were made about the tree calling him a murderer, screaming for help, threatening to call 911. But the jokes ended when the same friends visited Jeed's apartment to find the tree still standing on the patio in the same Christmas tree stand in March, in April, and even into May. They wanted to know what he had done to preserve the tree. "I talk to the angels that oversee trees," he had answered honestly. "Each day I bless the tree and thank it for its beauty." It took some convincing to assure his friends that the tree on his patio was indeed the leftover Christmas tree. For three years in a row he kept his Christmas trees until they died, usually in the spring. Then he would hold a ritual, cutting up the tree into parts and burning it in the barbecue. He would then take the ashes and distribute them back into nature, completing the circle of life. The fourth year, he found he could no longer cut live trees. They had become too dear to him. His ritualizing, cutting, and burning of these Christmas trees had made them seem far more than mere evergreens. They had become reminders of the grand web connecting all of creation. He found he could take nothing in life for granted, especially people.

After meeting Malidoma, Jeed had found even greater treasure in nature, life, and creation. Even the stones could become wise teachers. The recognition of other beings, spirit beings, in everyday events took away the egotistical notions that humanity was the center of the universe or that each of us is an island. These days, he consciously acquainted himself with the fullness of life, never feeling alone nor abandoned. Angels no longer occupied the same imaginary space as Santa Claus and fairy godmothers. Another world existed for him, a world of spirit companions, guardians, and other-dimensional beings.

As the two explorers wound their way to their secret destination, Rooster Rock peeked through the gathering clouds, perched in the middle of the Columbia. Like many other scenic wonders of the Gorge, its simplicity, harmony, and majesty could not be ignored. The Klickitat tribe had numerous legends regarding this area. The three volcanic peaks flanking the Gorge — Mount Hood, Mount Saint Helens, and Mount Adams — stood at the center of the legends. The Klickitat told how the Great Spirit had placed a stone bridge over the Columbia River as a symbol of peace between the Klickitat people to the north and the Multnomah people to the south. This stone bridge they called the Bridge of the Gods. Two brothers — Klickitat and Wyeast — led the two tribes which Great Spirit had separated to stop them from quarreling. Of course, even after having been separated, these brothers continued to quarrel, and were punished. Great Spirit took away the sun, leaving both tribes without fire. After they had repented, Great Spirit went to an old woman named Loo-wit, who had been the only one who had refrained from wrongdoing. She alone possessed fire. When Great Spirit told her he would grant her anything if she shared her fire with the penitent tribes, she asked for youth and beauty, and he granted her both. She placed her fire on the Bridge of the Gods so both tribes would have warmth in their lands once again. But the two brothers became enamored with the beautiful woman who had given them fire. They began to desire her and then quarrel over her, returning to their warring ways. The peoples of the two tribes began once again to war, and Great Spirit grew very angry. He destroyed the sign of peace, the Bridge of the Gods, causing it to crumble into the Columbia. He then changed the two brother-chiefs into mountains — Wyeast became Mount Hood and Klickitat became Mount Adams. Loo-wit he also changed into a mountain, but a youthful and beautiful mountain — Mount Saint Helens. Over the centuries, the brothers have continued their feud by throwing rocks at one another and spewing forth lava. They stand as reminders for all generations as to the consequences of choosing selfishness, greed, and war over oneness, compassion, and peace. In our modern times, it appears Loo-wit has grown weary of the feuding and made her own statement. In more ways than one, the Feminine will no longer stand by and watch patriarchal attitudes create strife.

The tale of the quarreling brothers reminded Jeed of statements he had heard from Malidoma's friend, author Robert Bly, in his book *Iron John*, regarding the ever-growing problem of gangs in our society. Malidoma looks at our modern culture from the perspective of his own indigenous culture, where such problems do not exist, and states point blank that the reason why we have gang problems in our society is because we do not initiate our young men into manhood. We are a country of absent fathers where the average time spent with a child is between seven and fifteen minutes per day. That's it. Fathers in America spend more time in the bathroom grunting on the toilet and pissing away their lives than they spend talking with their sons. And it shows. Bly adds to Malidoma's observations by stating that a boy who is not *shown* his manhood moves into what Bly calls his Shadow Wildman, a destructive and rebellious behavioral pattern that demands attention not previously provided. These are our gangs, pure and simple. These are boys moving into men's bodies who wreak havoc across personal boundaries because their fathers never took the time to show them boundaries. And the most important boundary to a male is the boundary that delineates where the boy leaves off and the man begins.

Jeed looked over at Josh and wondered whether Malidoma and Bly were correct. After all, Chris loved to spend time with his boys. But once they got into high school, something had changed. They seemed to have inherited his own sense of busyness. None seemed to have time for the other. Even Jane worked at the family-owned store. It was not uncommon to spend most nights eating in a restaurant or ordering takeout. Would Chris's effort to initiate his youngest son into manhood have any impact?

Josh's head began to droop, first to the left and then to the right. His jaw sagged open. The journey had already taken a toll on him. Would he last the day? Off in the distance, Jeed spied the legendary promontory that lived up to its name. Beacon Rock jutted above the Columbia like a sentinel lighthouse. Towering more than 900 feet straight into the air, the rocky giant resembled a broken pillar from some ancient, demolished temple. Recognized as a geological wonder by archaeologists, the craggy minaret proved to be a site of spiritual wonder as well among shamans and eco-spiritualists alike. A couple of times already, Jeed had climbed the precarious trail that zigzagged back and forth to the top of the west face. Each time he had been filled with a different kind of awe. So many different combinations of scenery could be witnessed: sensational seasonal colors of vegetation, parades of weather, migrating birds or raptors, or wildlife traversing the river. No two visits ever brought the same experience. Jeed had picked this place for its unpredictability, and he was looking forward to what mystery might unfold during this current trek.

Like the surrounding mountains, Beacon Rock also carried legends. Like Wyeast and Klickitat, Beacon Rock and Rooster Rock had once been brothers arguing over a maiden. In this case, it was Coyote who had changed the brothers into rocks for their quarreling. The maiden had been turned into Horsetail Falls, which the sojourners presently were passing. *Too bad Josh is missing this*, Jeed thought. Should he wake him? No, there might still be an opportunity on the way back. Beacon Rock ranks as one of the largest monoliths in the world. How odd that so much rich legend in this area has to do with quarreling men. Though women had been the object of these quarrels, it was not lost on Jeed that the women most likely served as archetypes for Mother Earth herself. How long had men used the Earth as an object of their own desires, to be exploited for their own pleasures? Odd that the pulp mill served as the western entrance into the Gorge. Beacon Rock stood as a gravestone, an epitaph as it were, to an inevitable end of a people who cannot find harmony among themselves and with nature. The Bridge of the Gods had served as a symbol of peace, a monument to the ways of people who once remembered their sacredness and heard the Great Spirit within. To those who have forgotten these ways, there remain only crumbled rocks and legends as to what might have been.

As Jeed pulled his little Samurai jeep into the parking area off the road, Josh roused from his slumber, eyes wide open. After turning the ignition off, Jeed just sat for a few moments in silence. Because it was a Tuesday, and a damp, cold, Pacific Northwest December day, no other cars huddled against the giant rock, which pleased Jeed. The wind had begun to howl through the trees interspersed among the many rocky outcroppings. Rain fell erratically as if the clouds couldn't decide whether to bluster or yield to the wintry sun — so typical of a day in the Gorge. Without a word, Jeed exited with Josh following him to the back of the vehicle. Opening the rear door, Jeed slipped on his gloves, zipped up his parka, and tied the hood tightly around his head. He knew the wind and rain most likely would not let up, and would probably intensify with the changing weather. Finally breaking his silence, he decided to ask Josh, "Did you bring any rain gear?" wondering if Josh had dressed warmly enough.

Staring at his feet, Josh wondered if he should break his silence. A whim danced in his eyes as he tried to decide whether to return to the world of conversation and exchange. The silence had given him time to lose his frustration and anger. The quiet had left him with a new sense of peace about himself. He felt different. Proud how he'd endured this strange journey and moved through his fear and panic. He did not want to lose this peace by using words.

"Just what I have on," he finally surrendered.

"Do you have anything to protect your head?"

"Just my stocking cap."

"You'd better put it on. You will need as much protection as you can get. There is an umbrella over there above the wheel well. You are welcome to take it if you wish." The old golfing umbrella, an orange and black monstrosity, worked well in the city or on the golf links. But out here it could prove to be as much a burden as a blessing. Jeed purposefully decided not to make a recommendation one way or the other, for he wanted Josh to seek his own choices and make his own decisions this day. The lad stared at the offering for a moment.

"No. That's OK. I'll use what I have." With a snap he flipped his stocking cap over his head, swung his pack on his back, and stood silently waiting for directions to God-knows-where. From the road, the trail hid from view. Jeed watched Josh wonder if they were going to attempt to climb up this wall of rock, and if so, how.

"I'll lead the way. Even though I still encourage silence, don't hesitate to say anything if you need help of any kind or you need rest. You should be mindful of yourself and let me know if you are in need."

"OK." Whatever Jeed was about to do, Josh would follow. Trust seemed his only comfort at this point.

A mixture of feelings rattled inside Jeed. A part of himself, the part who was godfather, wanted to hug his godson and let him know everything would be fine. But there reigned another part — the Initiator, Bringer of the Mysteries of Manhood, the Hierophant — who wanted transformation for his charge. Would conflicting feelings for the Boy interfere? Would the trepidation of the Boy yield to the sense of adventure within the Man? They were about to find out.

After retrieving one of two packs he'd brought along, Jeed slammed the door, locked it, and headed toward the trailhead hidden behind the firs. Josh followed. Without looking back, Jeed marched with crisp footsteps through the woods to the base of the giant monolith. The trail began steeply from the start. They hiked fifteen feet, turned 180 degrees and hiked another twenty feet, and turned again, stepping upon rock stairs anchored in place with cable and cement. Back and forth, back and forth they trudged; higher and higher they climbed. Where rock ceased, trailblazers from years gone by had erected wooden trestles and bridges, which spanned chasms and dead ends. Jeed's legs began to ache as they continued the climb. Listening carefully for any hint of what was going on behind him, he never turned to look. As they rose high above the ground, the wind grew louder and louder, whipping both with cold raindrops. "Back," Brother Wind seemed to howl "Turn back. This is the realm of spirits and men. Return this boy to his mother's arms. Go back."

At this point, Jeed could hear Josh panting wildly. Up ahead, some five more tiers, lay a resting spot he loved to use for meditation and rejuvenation. The panting behind him began to fade. Still, he didn't turn around. *Josh must ask for what he needs.* Even though Jeed's footsteps slowed a bit, there burned within him a determination not to coddle the Boy, nor transgress the boundaries of the Man. Jeed had to be invited, not intrude in this world of the Man, and Josh needed to recognize those boundaries within himself. Finally, just as Jeed was about to buckle with uncontrollable concern, he heard Josh gasp, "Jeed. Jeed. Wait."

The wind laughed with a rippling, bubbly sound around Jeed's parka as he turned. Josh lay on the ground, holding his side, grimacing with pain. Trying not to appear motherly or fatherly, Jeed hiked back down to the bottom of the terraced ledge and knelt beside his ward. "What's wrong? You OK?"

"My side aches something horrible." The fasting had taken its toll. He needed rest for a while so his guts could satisfy his screaming organs' want for food. The rain seemed to let up for a moment as if in sympathy.

"Here, let me see if I can't get the pain to ease up." Josh lifted his jacket enough for Jeed to place his hands over his aching left side. From the time Josh had been a boy, he had witnessed his godfather's ability to make things better with his laying on of hands, whether it was fixing his dad's backaches or his mom's stiff necks or his own sore joints while growing up. Though Josh never understood this ability, he had grown to trust it.

As Jeed palpated the aching area, he could tell the lad needed to calm down. "Josh, I want you to breathe deep and easy. When you breathe out, I want you to see the pain going out with your breath." After the first few breaths, Josh began naturally inhaling and exhaling with what is termed yogic breathing. A smile flickered on Jeed's face as he knew the pain would leave in short order.

As they rested, both gazed over the astonishing beauty unfolding below them as the clouds began to lift more and more, exposing the cliffs, waterfalls, and escarpments of the Gorge. What had seemed like a gray tomb only minutes earlier now transformed into a pastoral painting on which the eyes feasted. *No wonder legends abound in this area*, Jeed thought. The panorama had turned magical.

"Ready to continue?" Jeed prompted, pulling Josh back from his trance as he gazed spellbound at the river below. The question seemed to awaken the wind as well. As Jeed stood, the wind once again whipped at his parka hood, rippling and bubbling with sound. *Capricious laughter of the gods*, he thought. Brother Wind seemed protective of the rock tower, still wishing to turn back the undeserving. "Why bring a boy to the realm of the gods?" it whispered in Jeed's mind.

"Yeah, I'm ready," Josh smiled back, not wanting to show his embarrassment for not being able to keep up with an old man.

"Don't feel embarrassed, Josh. 'The strongest man is he who fears not his weakness.' Embrace that part of yourself. You did the right thing in calling out. We are all here to help one another. If a man tries to hide his weakness, he becomes ruled by the very fears he tries to hide. Remember, it's the king who is ruled by the kingdom. Not the other way around. The lowly serf is the strongest man in the kingdom because he has nothing to lose, and everything to gain by being himself."

Pondering these thoughts, Josh stared out over the vastness of the Gorge. Then, standing up and brushing himself off, he looked at Jeed and pronounced, "I'm ready."

"It's not much further to the top. We won't be stopping again."

In spite of the wind, Jeed heard a mumbled, "Thank God."

Back and forth they trekked up one level to another, over more bridges and trestles until they stepped off onto an island of vegetation. What had been a ledge merged into a trail. Jeed picked up the pace, wanting to leave Josh farther behind. With his head bent down, staring unconsciously with each step, the lad missed the quickening pace. As Jeed turned the bend into the trees, he dropped out of sight. From this point the trail spiraled another hundred feet in altitude. Surrounded by brush and trees, little could be seen except the top edge itself. Ascending the final section of trail, Jeed noticed Josh straggling farther behind. The wind whistled and blustered at the unprotected top, swirling once again with laughter, as if from the ancient spirits who had tried to bring peace to man. Pulling himself up the final two boulders before arriving at the plateau, Jeed spied what he had been anticipating. Sitting on his haunches, he waited for Josh's arrival. Filled with giddiness, he extended his hand to help the exhausted straggler up the boulder.

"That's OK. I got it," Josh announced, his words partially lost against the clatter of Jeed's flapping hood. As the two stood and climbed the final section of trail, they noticed two men with their backs to them, staring over the panorama. Jeed ambled over, approaching them with bravado, and swung his arms around the necks of both. They turned. Paul and Chris smiled smiles as big as the Gorge. The wind had teared Chris's eyes. Proudly he stared at his younger son, knowing how tough the climb had proved to be.

"Dude!" Josh said as his mouth dropped open. He stood motionless trying to figure out how they had beaten him to the top. They must have broken speed limits driving down from Seattle. "God! I should have known," he yelled. Delight began to overwhelm him. With a broad grin, he stumbled over and began laughing, bear-hugging all three conspirators, who surrounded him in their circle of manhood. The spirits must have been pleased.

Chapter Nine

RITUAL OF EARTH AND SKY

*T*his is incredible." Chris gestured with arms fully spread-eagle before the Gorge. "Have you ever seen anything like it?" To the west they could see as far as Portland, some twenty-five miles as the crow flies. To the east they could see as far as the river bend, flanked by all the sites from which legends had sprung. Like the Bridge of the Gods, these men of of the modern day connected the two worlds of the ancient and the modern, worlds of quarrelsome men trying to find peace with nature and one another. Perhaps this day would please the gods who had once tried to bring peace to this region.

Paul, too, shook his head in disbelief over the stunning panorama. Hands stuffed in pants pockets, trying to maintain some protection against the bite of the cold wind, he paced back and forth to get his circulation pumping. His coat might have worked nicely in Seattle, but here its cloth covering might as well have been made of fishnet. Jeed realized he had failed to tell these two how to dress for the climb. Chris sported a Panama hat, which did nothing for his ears. At least his balding head was covered.

"What's that over there?" Chris pointed across the river.

"Oh, that's Crown Point. It's a tourist observation site built long ago by the Army Corps of Engineers. It's made completely of stone from the surrounding area. Quite a view from there. In more ways than one." On the other side of the river, a couple miles to the west, the stone building stood like a small castle on a mountaintop. Overlooking Rooster Rock, which sat solidly below in the Columbia, the observation telescopes proved quite popular in the summer, having a prime view of the nude beach on the north side of Rooster Rock State Park.

Josh kept commenting how he should have figured out the surprise. All the little hints he had wondered about, all the fuss about whose car to take to the train station. What he didn't know was that as the train had left the station in Seattle, Jane had driven up in the van to meet Chris and Paul — all their necessities loaded into Paul's car, hugs exchanged, with the two men taking off like bats out hell down Interstate 5, trying to beat the train to Portland. Josh soaked in the reverie of all the trouble that brother and father had gone to, all the caring conveyed in their standing on top of a rock spire, 900 feet in the air, delighted as a bunch of tourists. The silence had been broken, and the moment felt sweet.

Jeed cleared his throat. Like the silence, the time had come to break up the tourist convention. "OK guys, I think it's time for us to continue."

There's more? Josh wondered to himself. *Now what?*

"Josh, I'd like you to sit over there on the boulder facing east. Paul, if you would stand to my right facing south. Chris, you stand on my left facing north. And I shall face west." All took their places. The wind began kicking up again, swirling wildly. Jeed pushed his parka hood off his head, lowering it as he thought. The chill of the wind made his ears ring. Shivering and not knowing why, Jeed began his introit.

"Josh, we have all come together here with you so that we might welcome you into your manhood. This is not something we take lightly. We have come with open hearts to speak our truth and to witness this event today. We ask your angels and your spirit guides to be with us, to guide us, to watch over us as we try to awaken in you the power of your manhood. We invite any other spirit helpers of highest good to be with us this day as we begin this ritual of initiation." Goose bumps rose on Jeed's arms and legs. One of the essentials he had learned from Malidoma was that there is no ritual without the invocation, or invitation to the spirit realm. Otherwise, men stand alone in ceremony. There is honor in admitting our need and our communion with the Otherworld. For we are beings who are part of the grand Oneness, who are never alone. Indeed, no man is an island. And no man can lay claim to his manhood by thinking of himself as an island.

"Does anyone else wish to invite any other spirit beings into our presence?"

Paul answered immediately, "I would like to invite Uncle Frank to be here with us. I know he would like to be a part of this with us."

Chris nodded his head approvingly. "I would like to invite the spirit of the Eagle, who guides me and helps me see my path clearly, who gives me courage to be myself." Chris looked over at his youngest son, wishing him courage to be himself as well. Josh took it all in stride, having witnessed many times his father's studying and practicing of Native American spirituality. Chris had even studied with a Lakota shaman in the Seattle area, finding comfort in the knowledge of what the Lakota call "power animals." Others call these spirit beings "oversouls," and yet others, like Dorothy Maclean, consider these oversouls to be one more aspect of the angelic realm. No matter what name or metaphor one uses, a rose is a rose. Ritual works from whatever perspective one chooses to recognize as long as one's spiritual consciousness and one's intention first create the space for these spirit beings and then hold the space as the unexplainable unfolds. These beings care not how we choose to see them. They simply are.

Turning toward Chris, Jeed asked, "Would you open our ritual space with your spirit-calling song?" Chris had been given the sacred song in a dream a year ago. In the dream, a Native medicine man had sung for him the mysterious words, telling him to use the song to call in the beings of the other realms. For months he had checked with linguists at the University of Washington and elsewhere to ascertain their meaning. The end of his search came with the finding of an old Lakota Sioux Elder, who explained that the words came from an ancient Sioux language no longer spoken. However, the language still existed in ancient songs and chants handed down from Lakota ancestors. The Elder told Chris not to reveal the meaning of the song, for it would dilute its power. With this in mind, Chris closed his eyes, entered into himself, and took a deep breath. With solemnity he began to sing above the wind, strongly and clearly. His voice, with its deep basso tones, sang for his son, sang for his manhood, calling in the beings who would show wisdom, kindness, and favor upon him. No sooner had he finished the first line than the wind subsided immediately. Instead of the noise of a rushing gale through the trees below, there arose a warming stillness, not unlike the dead calm before a tornado hits. The quieter the surroundings, the louder Chris sang. Over and over he chanted the lines of his spirit-calling song, tears streaming down his face. A sense of awe moved Jeed to bow his head in respect. He could feel the presence, could feel a lump in his throat. Chris, fighting for control of his own emotions, sang the closing line with quivering lips. He, too, had noticed the quelling of the wind and felt the power of the spirit-calling. The spirits would bless his son. He knew it. As the last note of the song lingered in the hushed air, all stood spellbound, Josh's eyes burning red with affection. No sooner had the last note died than the wind erupted once again, gusting and dancing on the plateau. Below, the fir trees once again turned into a thousand tiny whistles. Josh sat on the boulder as if he, too, had been chiseled of stone. The power of the ritual embraced him.

As Chris wiped at his eyes, Paul and Jeed stood motionless, no longer feeling the coldness of the wind. In fact, a warmth surrounded them as if the forces of nature had embraced them as companions.

Josh still sat frozen in place, staring into nothingness. New words flooded Jeed's mind.

"Josh, let me be the first to speak the words. I no longer see you as a boy. You are no longer your father's son. You are a man in the brotherhood of men. Hear these words. From this day forward I will acknowledge you as a man. I do this not only because I feel it important, but also because you yourself have taken the first steps into manhood. You have displayed acceptance of responsibility. You have also pursued self-knowledge, independence, and compassion toward others. We have all watched as your journey, that which we call life, has taken a turn. That turn is a turn away from the ways of a boy. You have taken on the mantle of manhood. And we are here to acknowledge that in you and with you.

"On your journey down here, I gave you several questions to ponder or write about. One of those was to have you describe Josh-the-boy and then Josh-the-man. Could you read or demonstrate to us what you wrote or drew or realized about Josh-the-boy?"

With the movements of a cat, Josh reached for his pack and opened the flap, revealing his journal. The pages flapped in the wind as he opened to the page where he had written words. "I didn't write very much," he confessed, almost apologizing. Straining their ears, the menfolk heard the words of the boy being read. Josh blushed as he read. Paul smiled as he heard the words referring to the teasing and fighting the two of them had engaged in over the years. Paul felt reassured to hear his brother speak in terms that were lighthearted, for Paul had never taken any of the squabbles seriously. Even when Josh had accidentally bloodied Paul's lip or caught him a good one in the family jewels, Paul had only pretended to be outraged. But inside, he felt the importance of their warrior play, the testing of strength and toughness. Such rough play prepared one for life. Josh had been so puny and slight as a young boy that Paul felt more like a guardian than an older brother. Even when friends would throw fits when their younger brothers wanted to tag along with them, Paul had welcomed Josh into his company. Within Paul dwelt an inherent calling not only to watch over his skinny little brother but to teach him, show him he

127

could bounce his wiry body against his big brother's bulk and power, and not be the worse for it. And here his little brother sat, now acknowledging him in kindness and respect for the last time as a boy. How odd to even think of his baby brother as a man, as an equal.

Chris smiled broadly, trying not to laugh out loud as Josh continued reading about the boy. The words from the journal plunged into Chris's heart, for he understood that his younger son had lived a childhood that Chris himself had never lived. Josh had not only been his son through those years, he had also been his playmate, had helped Chris to experience his own vicarious childhood. As a father, Chris had shown wisdom in allowing himself the luxury of sharing that childhood with Josh without robbing Josh of his own uniqueness, his own joys. Sure, Chris's outrageous shenanigans could burst forth like a jack-in-the-box at the most unexpected times, causing many to wonder who was younger, Chris or Josh. But there were those special times in which he included his younger son in his adult life as well.

When Josh decided to become a Cub Scout, following in the footsteps of his older brother — who had become the most decorated Cub Scout in the pack — Chris did more than encourage Josh. Chris actually volunteered to become cubmaster of the pack. He had watched carefully as Paul had dazzled his way through the stages of advancement through the previous years, helping him at every opportunity in learning knots, participating in community cleanup projects, and attending awards banquets that inevitably bestowed more honors upon his elder son. Through his boyhood, Paul actually had become Chris's way-shower, giving him social opportunities to understand and interact with his own inner child. But Josh was different. Chris had invested himself in Josh's life by taking a leadership role that not only benefited his younger son, but also benefited every other boy in the pack. How wild to have a cubmaster who could not only lead but also would put on clown suits, devise the most spectacular skits, and dream up the grandest ceremonies ever to amaze the Cub Scouts and their parents. Chris had become a legend because of his sons.

As Chris hung on every word read from Josh's journal, he realized he not only was listening to Josh's boyhood, but to his own as well. As Josh read the last line of Josh-the-boy being afraid to die, Chris's smile tightened. He remembered his brother Frank, who had committed suicide, and the profound impact that event had on Josh. Frank had been more afraid of living life than of greeting death. Chris said a silent prayer to Frank as Josh sat quietly, readying himself to read the next section. *Frank, if you are listening, I hope you are here to help out. This is also for you. I know how you thought the world was a painful and uncaring place. I want you to see how we are trying to change that. I hope you will be able to help Josh avoid the mistakes you made, as well as help him to face life in ways you couldn't.*

"Josh-the-man." The words interrupted Chris's thoughts. Again he focused on his son's words which reminded him of his own anxieties growing up. However, Josh did not display the fear that had ruled Chris during puberty. Josh had grown up learning how to conquer his fears, something Chris had never been taught. He peered at Paul, noticing a kind of smirk on his face. How much his oldest son had changed. He seemed wise beyond his years. The look on his face spoke its own words: "This is too cool." How well the mantle of manhood rested upon his younger brother. When had he grown up so suddenly? The words from the journal spoke with humility and compassion. Paul approved.

The last line of Josh-the-man snapped everyone to attention: "One last thing I notice is that I am STARVING!" All eyes soaked in the broad grin flashing across his face. Chris felt sympathy for Josh who had not known hunger before. Paul had also fasted the whole morning, causing Chris's sympathy to extend to both sons.

Hearing Josh's words left Jeed feeling admiration for his charge's courage at self-examination. The exercise of having him spend time looking within himself while on the train had proven to be no wasted effort. Seeing how the lad had taken the exercise seriously and listening to how he had found the positive potential in his approaching manhood pleased Jeed. "Josh," he said. "In the letter I wrote to you, I also asked you to listen for an inner voice. Were you able to hear that voice within?" This was a key question even though Jeed had no idea where it might go.

Josh's face wrinkled as he tried to find the right words. "Well, I couldn't hear anything. I wasn't sure what I was supposed to be listening for. But I did feel kind of strange when I asked for the voice to speak to me. I felt like I was somebody else, yet still me. Felt weird. I don't know if that's what you were talking about or not."

"Yes, exactly," Jeed cheered. "Well done. That is one of the ways this voice speaks to us. We feel as if we are in a different place, sometimes even in a different reality. Sometimes we feel like we do when we first wake up. The voice isn't always heard. Each of us has a special focus, a special talent, a special way we notice our environment or remember things. Some people can remember something if they hear it, others if they see it, and still others if they feel it or can write about it. Each of us has our own way of orienting our awareness. Yours is feeling. Your dad's is hearing. Mine is seeing. If I see something, I am much more aware of it than if I hear about it. I can remember much better if I see something rather than if I hear something. That's why I'm so bad at remembering people's names. If your dad hears a song, he remembers it forever. To this day I can't remember songs. Paul's awareness is oriented around a combination of sound and touch. That's why he is so good at the piano. So you see, you will have to learn more about these 'feelings' you have, and the way they speak to you. You'll have to learn when to trust them and when not to. You will learn how these feelings have an entire language, how they will make you aware of your surroundings in a way people are not normally aware of."

A tiny grin crept across Josh's face as if he didn't know whether to believe these words or not. "Give it time," Jeed counseled. "You will learn more about the voice as you grow older. I will teach you more in the coming years. Growth is a never-ending process. Do you have any questions about any of what has happened?"

Josh shook his head no. Because Josh-the-man had already addressed the matter of his fears in the reading from his journal, Jeed decided to skip to the final question for this part of the ritual. "Also in the letter I asked you to examine your own giftedness. You spoke about some of that in your journal. But are there any other aspects of yourself you find to be a gift? And how do you find that different in Josh-the-boy and Josh-the-man?"

Staring down at his hands as if examining dirty fingernails, Josh replied, "Well, I feel more self-confident now than I did as a boy. I think more of others and spend a lot of time talking to people, especially my friends, when they have problems or things that are bothering them. I seem to be good at that. I don't know why I'm so good at it, but everyone tells me I am."

Warmth filled Jeed as he stared at the vision of humility sitting cross-legged on the boulder. Only a man of wholeness is able to see his own value rather than wanting others to bestow value upon him. Jeed pondered over his own gross immaturity and sense of being lost when he was Josh's age. How he had resorted to attention-getting, how he had felt so alone because he had no clue who he was or what his purpose might be. Jane and Chris had been wise with their sons, making sure they had professional help at the first hint of low self-esteem was moving toward self-destructive statements. They had intervened before self-destructive words moved into self-destructive behavior, and their actions had paid off handsomely. The world would be a better place for Josh and Paul's presence, and Jeed stood filled with appreciation knowing he was about to play a role in helping Josh with his giftedness, his self-recognition, his wisdom as a man.

"When you were a boy, I used to tell you how special you were. Now that you have become a man, it is time to tell you why you are, indeed, blessed, Josh. All of us here feel it is important to acknowledge your manhood and dedicate ourselves to its furtherance. Much of our society is suffering from boys who are in men's bodies. Remember the pulp mill on the way here? Remember how it fouled the water and the air? Companies like that have been created by boys in men's bodies, who have little regard for the overall consequences of their actions. They assume precious little responsibility for the waste and the pollution they leave behind, which affects not only nature but also the human beings who live nearby. Their main concern is material gain. Unlike my Native American ancestors, they do not reflect on how their decisions and actions will affect the next seven generations. We must change that. From here on out, regard nature as your newly acquired mother. We are responsible to Mother Nature and Mother Earth, who nurture us. In the beginning, we acted as stewards and caretakers of the Earth. We watched over her and even helped heal her when needed. But we lost that purpose, surrendering to our own selfish needs for power, self-importance, greed, and dominance. We became a society of overlords instead of stewards.

"As you know, I come from Cherokee heritage. In Cherokee society I would be called an *adonisgi*, a medicine man or a holder of magic. Such men were responsible for opening gateways to the Otherworlds. In our culture, we would call this the supernatural world. But the Cherokee people, at one time, saw a bridge to the stars where the other realms existed. They saw no separation between the natural world and the supernatural world. These two realms connected seamlessly, never intended to be divided. The *adonisgi* possessed the powers of connection, oneness, known by some as the powers of the gatekeepers. These gateways served as bridges between other worlds, other dimensions. Originally, the Cherokee believed connection to be so sacred that they stood out among all tribes for their welcoming any race into the tribe, even the white race. Those of mixed blood they called the 'translators,' a sacred word honoring the abilities of these mixed bloods to connect two peoples, to translate their different ways from one to the other. The gatekeepers they honored as connectors or translators to the stars and to other worlds. All was meant to be in balance. Balance within self, balance between peoples, balance between different worlds.

"At one point, the *adonisgi* used their powers and knowledge of the sacred ways to bring healing to the Earth as well as to the people. And the Earth was kept well; all of life was in balance. But that changed. After the white man conquered the Cherokee, the people turned away from their *adonisgi* because their medicine, their powers, their magic, could not heal the white man's diseases that had descended upon them. The ancient ways of the *adonisgi* could not address the new vibrations, the strong forces, the new powers of the white nation. The Great White Father and the invading missionaries told the Cherokee that the old ways were heathen and uncivilized. They must separate the old from the new, the civilized from the uncivilized, the natural from the supernatural. When the Cherokee turned away from their medicine men, they also turned away from healing the Earth, leaving the powers of the white nation to decimate the Earth as it had the Cherokee.

"This story repeated itself time after time across the continent as America became a mighty nation. Today we watch as the oceans begin to choke and the forests fade. We must change all of this by changing ourselves. As you begin to own your manhood, your generation must once again learn not only the ways of the caretaker but also the ways of the steward. You must be ready to own your powers you have been blessed with to heal yourself, those around you, and even Mother Earth. This is no small matter. Your becoming a man is extremely important. Not only for you but also for the Earth."

Chris and Paul stood quietly with their heads bowed. Josh's expression had changed completely from one of near-amusement to one of solemnity. He had felt the words in his heart, and their truth resonated within his soul. Yes, these children of the New Earth must move from being children to becoming teachers, way-showers, and fully empowered men and women.

"I have no more to say at this time," said Jeed. "Does anyone else wish to say anything?"

"Yeah, I do," responded Chris, clearing his throat. All eyes turned as he retrieved his hiking pack hidden behind one of the larger boulders to the side. A cardboard poster tube protruded through the top of the pack. Just as Chris rejoined the group, there came the sound of voices below. They had visitors. A chance had always existed that others might be in the area, but the time of year, along with the weather, had made that possibility somewhat remote. All eyes turned to Jeed as if to ask *Now what?* He just shrugged his shoulders and uttered quietly, "I don't think they'll stay long. Let's wait it out." One part of him felt as if the ritual space had been invaded, but another part knew there were no coincidences, and consequently looked forward to what might unfold.

Two heads popped above the rock outcropping leading to the plateau. Two guys in their thirties looked as surprised as did the circle of four men. Both visitors had dressed warmly for the occasion: ski caps, gloves, and good parkas. The guy in the navy blue parka had eyes that darted about, as if looking for mischief. The other fellow wore teal green, making his reddish beard stand out even on this gray day.

"Hi!" said the man with the darting eyes. "We didn't expect anyone to be up here on a day like this." The wary part of Jeed wanted to ignore the cheerful greeting completely. But the curious part returned the greeting.

"Hi backatcha," he said begrudgingly. "Yeah, it's not exactly a great day for hiking." He gazed at his companions, his face reddening at the thought of how their circle must appear, sitting in forced silence, still holding the heightened emotions from the ritual. Jeed began to feel concern for bringing Josh here. But as he looked over at the silent figure, it was apparent that Josh was as amused as the man with the darting eyes.

"Christ! It's freezing-ass cold up here," said Darting Eyes. "Is the wind blowing right through you?" he asked his fellow hiker with the red beard.

"It's cold, but I like the wind," Red Beard responded.

"Well, I'm freezing my ass off." Darting Eyes wrapped his arms around himself and lifted one leg up, almost squatting as he tried to wrap it around the other. A grin emerged on Jeed's face as he began to figure out the puzzle of this interruption. "What in hell are you guys doing up here?"

Paul answered with a silent smile; Chris kept his back to the intruders. Clearing his voice, Jeed offered an excuse. "The scenery is incredible. There's nothing like it. Where you guys from?"

134

"Seattle," said Red Beard. "He's from Vancouver. I'm visiting."

"Aren't you guys freezing your asses off up here?" Darting Eyes asked Jeed.

Jeed stood rapt in contemplation as to what this scenario really meant, why these men had shown up out of the blue. In his studies with Malidoma, Jeed had studied the Way of Wyrd, an ancient form of spirituality that believed all of life to be connected. True to his Cherokee roots, Jeed was determined to discover what the Wyrd was trying to tell or teach or warn by bringing these two characters into sacred space. Perhaps what Josh needed to witness was the holding of sacred space. Oftentimes in life, places of beauty are intruded upon by those wish to visit the beauty but do not respect it. How often had Jeed seen natural hot springs carefully protected and developed by naturalists and outdoors enthusiasts, only to be descended upon in the years following by high school or college parties wanting to bathe in the healing waters while swilling beer or smoking pot or creating havoc? In their states of celebration, they would leave behind cans, bottles, trash, and discarded clothing, leaving those who cared about and monitored the hot springs to clean up after them. Could they keep these kids out? Should they? Most were under the legal drinking age. Should authorities be brought in to stop these midnight parties of destruction? Should the hot springs be guarded and reserved only for those who could commune with nature? In spite of trying different techniques to keep the "riffraff" out, the only option that finally worked was to educate and inform. Instructional signs were one of the means to inform the public. Naturalists and outdoor groups encouraged nearby schools to add environmental education about the public hot springs to their programs. Those who protected the hot springs began creating classes about the flora and fauna affected by the ecosystem, for which more and more visitors signed up. It took a few years, but the hot springs turned into a statewide and then national phenomenon because of the stewardship and caregiving started by the few. The many became aware of the prize they had. Parties still descended upon the hot springs at inappropriate times, but now the many felt empowered to inform the few of the consequences of their actions. All learned and all changed because of the interaction.

Jeed realized that the two intruders, in their own way, were providing Josh a lesson in holding space. To emphasize the point, Jeed leaned over to Chris and whispered, "We could finish the rest of the ritual in another spot. There's a log shelter over in the park area not far from here." Chris looked over at Josh, and shook his head no. He, too, knew the Way of Wyrd. He, too, understood that all were welcome, all had a purpose. He, too, joined Jeed in observing how this would turn out.

"Christ! I'm freezing my ass off up here. I don't know how you guys can take it." Darting Eyes stared at Red Beard. "Are you cold enough yet?"

Red Beard had a pleasant grin on his face as he took a deep breath. "Yeah, we can go. But I don't know of another place that has this kind of view. What a great spot." As the two turned to leave, Chris walked over to shake their hands, making a genuine comment about how nice it was to meet them, followed by a comical line about Darting Eyes's freezing ass. As the two began their climb down from the plateau, Jeed waited.

"God, I thought they were never going to leave," Paul said. "Sure was funny listening to them. Kind of like watching Laurel and Hardy."

"Indeed," began Jeed. "Paul, I've already taught you about the Way of Wyrd. Perhaps you could explain it to Josh. What do you think the Wyrd might have provided us here?" Paul thought about it a while, scratching his chin. After explaining to Josh the web of life and how it operates in the Wyrd, he began to describe how the Key of Silence allows us to hear all that's truly going on. When it came time to try and explain the interruption, he had to pause for a while. "Sometimes we can get too caught up in our own thing. Sometimes we need others to remind us that we are too serious. As much as I love everything that we are doing up here, I think it's good to remember that we also need to have fun. Those two guys came up here to have fun, enjoy the view. That's part of what this place is for.

And I think it's good to have that as part of our experience. Y'know, we need to make room for people who are different from us. And even though we have opened sacred space for our own purpose, I think it's good that others are welcome into that space to bring along what maybe we can't or aren't able to. It's like what you always tell me, Jeed. You can't have the sunrise without the sunset. I think these guys, in their own way, brought in some joy to make the seriousness and the sacredness even more special. It felt good to me."

"Yes. Sometimes we do take ourselves too seriously. Remember, Josh. Life is too important to take seriously." Jeed paused a moment to see if the humor landed. "We do have the power to create sacred space. And sometimes others come into that space uninvited. It's up to us how we see the intrusion. Do we pack up our tent and move to another campground? Or do we create welcome, and hold the intent as to why the space was created in the first place? Do we see the uninvited as invaders or as welcome guests? It's up to us how we choose to see any opportunity. Oftentimes, we see what we want to see rather than what actually may be there. So Paul recognized that these men provided a comic relief to the solemnity of the day. Your dad recognized that they were a reminder that all are welcome at our table. And I chose to see that they were teachers in disguise, helping us to provide you with one more opportunity to learn the mystery of manhood."

"Jeed," said Josh, "you're too weird." He smiled.

Josh looked over at his dad as Chris once again began fumbling in his pack. Delicately, he pulled forth the cardboard tube. With care he untied the tube and removed an object wrapped in teal flannel. As he unfolded the cloth, an arrow appeared. With reverence he held the arrow up in the wind with both hands. After turning to honor the four directions, he faced his son and spoke. "Josh, I have made this arrow for you and offer it as a symbol of this day. The arrowhead came from Priest Lake. I found it while diving in the waters one day. It represents to me the ancient ways and the ancient truths. Let it serve to remind you that you are a part of all our ancestors who have lived before us. They will watch over you as your spirit guides watch over you. They will speak to you if you wish to listen. They are a part of our souls as well as our bodies. The feathers come from an owl. I had to glue them on. So be a little careful."

Chris gently stroked the feathers with pride that reflected how much effort he had put into creating the arrow. The feathers hung elegantly on the shaft. "The owl is a symbol of wisdom, the kind of wisdom inherent in nature. It is a creature that is able to see in the darkness. Let it serve to remind you that you are never alone, that there are forces around you that can guide you along the path of light, even in times of darkness. The straight path is a path of light, straight like the Arrow of Light. As a man, you will be tried and tempted by others to take paths that are crooked. But you must trust the light that is in you; you must walk your own path. You cannot walk another's path any more than another can walk your path. As your father, I pray that you will be able to stay the true path and become the man you are meant to become." Chris handed the arrow to Josh, who accepted it as if it were made of eggshells.

"Thanks, Dad," he said in his most respectful tone. "You made the whole thing?"

"Except the shaft. I painted that. The feathers were a bit of a challenge," he chortled. "So you might be careful with them. It is a totem for you, to remind you of this day and to remember the true path of the Arrow of Light." It was not lost on Josh that "Arrow of Light" was the term for the Webelos symbol that is used in Cub Scouts when a Cub Scout graduates into Boy Scouts. Both sons knew how active Chris still remained in Scouting, continuing to help other boys the way he had helped the two of them. Though the symbol reminded both of a past they were leaving behind, the message remained pertinent for the rest of their days. The arrow may have seemed a bit nostalgic because of their own outgrowing Scouting, but both appreciated the effort their dad had shown. And they showed him honor in return.

Fumbling in his pack again, Chris retrieved a small bundle and began to unwrap it. As he untied the strings, he spoke. "In certain Native American traditions, there is a custom called 'the giveaway.'

The giveaway is a ceremony that is performed at a special occasion, such as the installing of a chief, where all the belongings of the new chief are given away to all in the tribe. Something is usually given in return. The giveaway is an interesting ceremony we would do well to understand. What it does is make the tribe one. It tells the tribe we are stewards, even of one another, that nothing is really ours. We just take care of it. Everything is a gift to be shared. I know now you are no longer just *my* son. You are your own man. You were given to me to take care of and to guide. And now I must give you away to the world."

Unwrapping the dark green cloth, Chris held up a stunning arrowhead necklace. The exquisite work, made of real tusk shells, bone beads, and fine leather, caught Josh's attention. Threads of maroon and forest green, Josh's favorite colors, were laced around the arrowhead and some of the shells. Chris had spent hours making the gift. Native artisans would have struggled to equal such craftsmanship, and it was a necklace that a warrior would be proud to wear. Chris's eyes reddened as he continued speaking. "As you know, this is the arrowhead you found on the beach at Priest Lake and gave to your Uncle Frank as a gift. After his death, it was the only thing you asked for from his belongings. You knew how much the arrowhead meant to me, so later you gave it to me as a gift to remember Frank by. I was deeply moved at the time. It told me how special you really are to live the giveaway in your heart without even knowing about it. Now, I give this arrowhead back to you as a part of this necklace. Accept it as a symbol of our oneness as men."

Josh accepted the memento and held it in his hand, staring at it for quite a while. Tears trickled down his cheeks. He could feel Uncle Frank there with him. He would treasure the gift always. Braving the cold, Josh pulled open his jacket and placed the leather cord around his neck. The arrowhead rested over his heart. It looked grand, something he would wear with pride and honor.

Thoughts flooded through Josh from all the times he had spent with Uncle Frank and Dad. His boyhood had been filled with joy because of these two child-hearted men. They had lived many

139

adventures with him and shared many laughs. Josh remembered how outraged he had gotten at Paul for his revealing that Uncle Frank was gay. The news had occurred over peanut butter and jelly sandwiches on a hike instead of during a family discussion. Josh's outrage had not arisen out of shame for Uncle Frank; the outrage had come from not having been trusted, not having been "in" on the secret. Frank had been terrified at the thought of what Paul and Josh might think of his lifestyle. The fear proved unfounded, but Josh still bridled at having been kept out of a secret. To him, secrets served no useful purpose. Frank had died, unable to share this moment, unable to hear how much Josh revered him, trusted him, and loved him. Josh had felt cheated. But now the arrowhead around his neck blazed like a memorial of unconditional love, unspoken, forever pointing at his heart.

Josh's emotions strained to be let out as he slipped off the boulder. Still holding the welling of feelings at bay, he leaned over and gave his dad a warm embrace. "Thanks, Dad. It's really fresh." Chris squeezed his eyes shut as he bear-hugged his younger son. But the tears leaked through, anyhow. He held his son-the-man as long as he could before Josh let go. Jeed watched breathlessly. Something in him felt ancient and free, beyond time, beyond space. He was watching a long-forgotten essence of the human condition — a part of ourselves that somehow wandered off through history. In this moment he no longer wondered about being worthy in adopting the role of Elder. In this moment he vibrated with the Elder who once guided us all. With human longing, Jeed wanted to freeze this moment, frame it, and display it in every hall of human conflict. *See!* it would say. *See how life used to be and can be once again? This is the force that binds all men. Lay down your ways of war, and remember your humanity. Remember. Come into remembrance. And never forget again.*

A gust of cold wind brought Jeed back into the mindfulness of the ritual. As Josh returned to his place on the boulder, Jeed turned to Paul. "Is there anything you'd like to say at this time, Paul?"

"No, not yet." He spoke haltingly as if fighting for the right words. The moment required true and strong words, but he could find none, yet. "I'll save all I have to say for a later time." Paul typically liked to pick his time and his place to say what he needed to say or do what he needed to do. He was a man who knew himself and knew what he wanted. Jeed could hardly wait to hear what he had up his sleeve.

"Josh, is there anything you want to say before we close this part of the ritual?"

"Yes," the initiate said matter-of-factly. "I understand what has been said here, and why we are together. But I still don't understand why I couldn't be told. Why was there all this secrecy? I hated it. Why couldn't I have been told?"

Jeed peered over at Chris, letting his friend know with his eyes that he would like to be the one to answer Josh. "Well, Josh, there is a reason. You are entering your manhood. You will soon enter life on your own. You will be entering a society that not only likes to keep secrets, you will also be entering a society that can take the profound and the sacred and destroy them. Secrets aren't so much the issue here. The real issue is trust. We had to test you to see if you would find us worthy of your trust. To have told you everything we had planned would have robbed you of the sacredness of it all. Some aspects of life are beyond words, and to try and contain those aspects with words only belittles them, even sometimes destroys it. Some things in life cannot be spoken of. They must only be lived. I believe that to be part of the lesson of the Wyrd when the two strangers showed up. They asked us what we were doing up here, and we chose not to tell them. Trust may have been part of the reason, but the real reason is that we wanted to maintain our sacred space. It was not meant to be shared with just anyone.

"There's another side of secrets — the dark side. Some secrets are kept in darkness. It's because some people do not want to stand in the light of truth. Those who plot against nature are men with kept secrets. We have to question whether this kind of man is worthy of trust. Certain men you must never reveal your sacredness to. Such men dishonor sacredness and dishonor those who hold sacred truths in their hearts. Wisdom is needed to know if a secret is being kept to hide the truth or being kept to honor sacredness. In such matters, wisdom is always needed. Wisdom comes only with growth, with age, with living life. We needed to know if you could trust us in what we were trying to do. In the future, you will have to learn well who you can trust and who you cannot trust with your truths. Trust is a very important gift. Once lost, it is almost never found again."

I'm confused, Josh thought to himself. *What is right can become wrong; what I thought wrong can be right.* He needed time to digest the torrent of information washing through him. The world he had known was escaping him, and he wasn't sure whether he cared for it or not.

"It's time to close our ritual space and head back down," Jeed urged. The climb had taken longer than he had gauged, and sometimes timing could prove threatening in the Gorge. As Chris sang his spirit song, this time sending the spirits back in gratitude and bringing closure to this meeting of earth and sky, the wind erupted in dance, kicking up sand and dead undergrowth. The bridge between two worlds had disappeared, not unlike the Bridge of the Gods. But the wind danced in the knowing that such bridges could be reopened, would be reopened. And Josh was about to find out how. The adventurers gathered their hiking packs and water bottles, readying themselves for the descent — a descent that would take them to yet another world.

Chapter Ten

RITUAL OF THE WATERS

*T*he symbol of Beacon Rock engaging the winds of the Gorge stood as a monument of blessing, a meeting of the forces of the heavens with the forces of the Earth. This connection of earth and sky, normally seen as the ever-changing weather crashing against the never-changing pillar of stone, had been transcended by the ritual. Two worlds had come together at the meeting of men, showing Josh the powers of connection. Such powers inherently rest within the hearts of the Children of the New Earth. But these children are taught by the ways of modern man to keep their hearts closed to nature, which has to be dominated, has to be ruled. Does the weather threaten the Beacon Rock? Does the Rock impede the progress of the weather? No. Each has its place. Even more important, those who know the powers of both had stepped into sacred space they themselves had opened in recognition of what happens when such worlds meet. And so it fell upon Jeed and Chris to revisit the ancient ways and merge them with the modern so that the heart of one of the

Children of the New Earth might open once again to greet the forces of Oneness, which transcend duality. Here amongst the clashing realms of the heavenly and the earthly they had encouraged one of these gifted ones to remember why he had been born. When the ever-changing and the never-changing meet, transcendence results. These Children of the New Earth carry within their hearts the secret of transcendence. They simply have to awaken to the secret, remember it. It remained to be seen whether Josh would move into Remembrance.

"Are we ready to go to the next location?" Jeed asked while they retraced their steps.

"You mean there's more?" asked Josh in near-exasperation.

"Yes, there's much more, Josh. From here we will now hike up to that mountain over there." Jeed pointed to the south where the banks of the Columbia rose quickly against the Cascade Mountains. "That's Hamilton Mountain. Not far from it is a waterfall we will reach, called Rodney Falls."

"How far is it?" Josh asked, wondering if his body was going to last.

"It's about a mile and a half, maybe a bit more. The trail may be a bit difficult because of all the rain. We'll have to see." Hamilton Mountain stood like a pyramid flanked on either side by ridges and cliffs. Josh stared in disbelief at the destination.

"I guess these old legs will get a workout," Chris chimed merrily, half laughing as he adjusted his hiking pack on his back.

"As we continue our hike down, I'd ask that we once again go into silence until we reach the next location. Talk only if you feel it's necessary. Does everybody have everything?" The silence indicated no turning back.

The climb down Beacon Rock proved to be almost as taxing as the climb up. Chris's body wasn't the only one complaining with soreness. The steep angle of the rocky path not only flexed little-used muscles, it also let them know the derivation of the term "tenderfoot." To accentuate the descent, clouds darkened overhead and let loose a torrent of rain. The raindrops became tiny spears stinging the men's faces, prodding them to move onward. No longer did the unexplainable warmth at the top surround them. Had the spirits abandoned them? Or were the spirits of nature in a hurry to unite once again with the spirit of man at the waterfall — waters from the heavens driving the men onward to the waters of the Earth?

Back and forth, step after toe-first step, the men wound their way down the craggy spire, the rain relentlessly pelting them, the wind howling once again against the cliffs. Jeed found himself mesmerized by the cacophony, trying to move into the Wyrd to sense any message from the Otherworld. His mind began to wander as his legs and feet shifted into automatic gear. Words drifted into his thoughts, words he had spoken: "Josh we are here to honor you." The phrase repeated in his mind over and over, footfall after footfall.

Jeed's memory moved back to a time when honor had been revealed to him in a way he had never dreamed. He had just left Mount Angel Seminary and didn't know what to do with his life. Strong emotions kept trying to pull him back to the abbey. But he knew he could not return unless something changed — whether he needed to change or the abbey needed to change, he couldn't determine. In either case, he had to figure out what truly had driven him away. Had it been the hypocrisy of spiritual pursuit pitted against spiritual conformity? Or did he simply not have the horses to plow through a lifestyle that demanded obedience for obedience's sake? He needed to find out. So with the logic of a mathematician, he figured out how long he should force himself to find the answer he sought. He knew too short of a time would allow his emotions to override his senses and pull him back to the dream he had sought throughout his boyhood — service to humanity. Because of his confrontation with the head monk of the minor seminary, he had realized that obedience without love was empty. How could monks who dedicated themselves to the Prince of Love be so unloving? Their minds could speak love but their hearts oftentimes echoed the emptiness of the abbey church at night. Yes, he needed to stay away from the abbey long enough to be objective about pursuing the priesthood. He should wait four years. But what to do during those four years? Go to college at a state university? That would take money he presently didn't possess. Why not the Air Force? Follow in his father's footsteps. Not only would he be forced to stay away from the abbey hill for four years, he'd have a paid education waiting for him at the end. Little did he know he would rue the day he made that decision, yet also give thanks for his inner wisdom.

Boot camp, which the Air Force euphemistically called "basic training," crashed against his fragilities from the seminary — a paper boat thrown into a raging river. His class of recruits (called a "flight") elected him chapel guide, which turned into a nightmare. As one of the chapel guides, Jeed marched the Catholic boys to and from church functions at Lackland Air Force Base, Texas. An antagonist — eager to bully — resented the attention paid to the peaceful Jeed, and kept looking for an opportunity to "whup his ass," oftentimes belittling him in front of the rest of flight. Jeed's innocence haunted him from the very first night in the barracks — while in the showers. The training instructor (TI) had given the entire flight fifteen minutes to shower under six shower heads. Naked bodies flew everywhere. Jeed lagged behind, not comfortable with his nudity. Laughter ensued as soapy skins rubbed up against one another, prompting stories about the mashed potatoes having been laced with saltpeter at the mess hall. In his innocence, Jeed had to ask, "What's saltpeter?" Many thought he was joking.

"You don't know what saltpeter is?" pressed those nearby.

"Well, I thought so," said Jeed. "Isn't it potassium nitrate?" Howls of laughter erupted, sending the entire flight into unending jokes. Only Jeed knew the actual meaning of the word. Saltpeter was indeed potassium nitrate, its common name coming from the French term meaning "salt of the rock." This early form of gunpowder originally was found in crusty deposits on rocks, having a crystalline appearance like salt. Why it would be put in the mashed potatoes was beyond Jeed. And what was so funny? If anything was funny, it was a bunch of grown men showering in a rugby scrum under the showers. He'd never seen such a sight.

The TI returned exactly sixteen minutes later, screaming warnings of dire consequences if he found any "swinging dicks" still in the shower. After ordering everyone into their bunks, he killed the lights. Everyone settled down into their bunks. One of the guys nearby whispered to Jeed, "Hey, Salt. Just so you know about the mashed potatoes; saltpeter is used to keep guys from getting horny. Keeps you soft." From that night forward, Jeed the chapel guide was nicknamed "Salt." From that night forward, something in him changed. Something that bullies or institutions could never touch. Would never touch. Never would he compromise who he was to be accepted by others. He realized who he was would always be good enough. The chapel guide was one of grunts.

Toward the end of boot camp, Jeed's TI and flight members nominated him to represent the flight in the competition for the American Spirit of Honor Medal. All flights in the same ten-week cycle of training were eligible to compete before a board of five officers. First, a written test had to be passed. Then, the panel of officers peppered each contestant individually with military trivia as well as examining their character, their uniforms, and their military training. Woe be it to anyone whose shoes were not blindingly spit-polished or whose salute did not follow exactly the line of buttons up and down his shirt. One single error would eliminate the most accomplished basic trainee. Great prestige fell upon the squadron commander and TI should a recruit of theirs win the medal. The competition had become legendary among the commanding officers. Bragging rights at the Officers Club got the notice of officers higher up in the chain of command.

A few officers had the reputation of multiple wins, and they let everyone else know it. When Jeed's TI realized his amazing memory, word spread rapidly to superiors. Past tests appeared out of nowhere. His TI allowed Jeed to skip KP, parade training, and any other drill in order to cram for the squadron competition. When Jeed appeared before the squadron commander to see who would win the next level of the competition, he fell prey to a trick question that would have eliminated him. But rather than admit defeat, Jeed went to logical extremes to circumnavigate his mistake, arguing with the commander, totally confusing him. In defense, Jeed pointed to a loophole in the way the commander had asked the trick question rather than admit he had screwed up. Flustered, the squadron commander dismissed him. When grilled for information by his TI upon his return to the barracks, he truthfully responded, "I'm sorry, I screwed up. Not only did I miss a trick question at the end, I made matters worse by going into a major line of bullshit, arguing how there were really two answers rather than one. The commander dismissed me." The TI broke into wild laughter. Jeed stood there flabbergasted waiting for the ax to fall.

Unmercifully, the TI then yelled, "Why the hell didn't you think things out clearly before answering?" All Jeed could do was blush. Rising slowly from his desk, the TI glowered at his shamed airman and extended his hand. "Congratulations. You beat out the others." A grin the size of Texas replaced the glower. "Now get yourself ready for the top competition. You've got a week. If you have to stay up all night to get ready, then do it. You have the run of the barracks as well as my office. You can go to the base library anytime you wish. Don't abuse it." Apparently, the squadron commander had been so impressed with Jeed's bullshitting that he felt it might come in handy for the basewide competition.

Over the next week, more copies of past tests appeared. More interview questions from past competitions found their way into Jeed's hands. He grew nervous as he read the competition regulations at the base library. Clearly, to have copies of these questions and past tests was considered cheating. And apparently, everyone cheated. But getting the medal was the end-all and be-all. Feeling the pressure to win, he crammed every night of the week, and studied military history at the library just in case the board of officers got creative in their questioning. Others took over his duties and his turns at base cleanup and KP. Jeed was treated like a king. Finally, the day arrived, his mind a boiling cauldron of military trivia.

After taking the written exam, Jeed waited his turn in the side room. Through the door he could hear the heel clicks, the military greetings, and the barking of answers of the other squadron winners. His nerves were those of a man waiting to be executed. The door opened. His turn to face the firing squad of questions. Gauging the distance from the door to the chair, where he would turn ninety degrees and salute, he measured each step while making sure his arms swung exactly the right distance, exactly the right angle, his chin tucked strongly against his neck. Three steps away, he realized he was going to miss the exact mark where he should stop and snap his heels together. Feeling awkward and totally clumsy, he altered his stride to hit his mark. He'd screwed up again. As he turned smartly a full ninety degrees, he blushed to the point of sweating. The wooden chair had become an electric chair, and he felt like dying. With staccato words he greeted the board with proper protocol. The lead officer invited him to sit. He wanted to become invisible. The questions began firing in machine-gun fashion. He barely heard himself speaking, still thinking on one level how he'd messed up from the start. He kept obsessing how he'd sabotaged his chances. And in the end came the most punishing question by the lowest-ranking officer.

"Airman, you seem very knowledgeable on a large range of topics we have presented you. It is quite impressive. Have you been coached in any way or given any cheat sheets?"

Jeed had never been any good at lying. But he was in automaton mode at this point. "No sir. I was given plenty time to stay at the library and given all the study time I needed to prepare." Which was a terrific half-truth. He couldn't exit the examining room fast enough, still calculating every step precisely. On the walk back to the barracks, he began to compose an apology to his TI. He had "fucked up" once again. Only this time he couldn't bullshit his way out of it. Honor. What a strange word when the mind is totally disconnected from the heart.

No sooner had Jeed walked into his TI's office than a tirade began about how he had been such a clown. The TI had been telephoned. Jeed apologized profusely, tried to explain he must have been more nervous than he realized, getting his feet all tangled approaching the chair and all. The TI's icy face sent shivers through him. With arms folded, the steely sergeant rose from his chair, staring at the lad with the strangest look. What planet had spawned such a creature as Jeed? And, just like before, he extended his hand, eyes quickly softening. "Congratulations, airman. You did it. You won the American Spirit of Honor Medal."

"Me?" Jeed gasped in utter disbelief. "How?" All he could think of was the lie at the end.

"Yeah, you. Do you know you are the only airman to serve under me in the last three years to win it?" From that day forward, Jeed's ass was made of gold, and the TI made sure everyone in the flight had better kiss it. At the end of the ten weeks of training, in front of the entire flight, the TI pulled out the graduation photo in one hand and a pair of scissors in the other. "You bunch of swinging dicks are the sorriest bunch of assholes I ever laid eyes on. You see this photograph? There is only one picture in here worth keeping." And he began snipping. After holding up Jeed's picture for everyone to see, he took the rest of the photo and tore it into shreds. That evening he tacked the tiny cutout on the barracks bulletin board with the words "Honor" and "Spirit" carefully written underneath.

Honor? Spirit? The American Spirit of Honor Medal — won by cheating? To this day, Jeed has the medal, the ribbon, and the citation locked away in his memorabilia chest. But not as a source of pride. He has it to this day to remind himself what honor and spirit should *not* be in America: winning at all cost. In the years following his stint in the Air Force, Jeed never forgot the lesson he had learned during those ten weeks at Lackland AFB. And he intended to pass that lesson on when he heard Josh reading from his journal at the top of Beacon Rock. For Josh had also spoken about honor and spirit, and for Jeed it made up for those days of cheat sheets and so-called military pride. Josh had a sense of true honor and how it stemmed from his exploration of the spiritual self. America and the world would do well to listen to these Children of the New Earth. For they know the difference between the kind of pride that lifts up the spirit and the kind of pride that tears down others, where the winner takes all, only to have it later turn to ashes in his hands.

As Chris and Jeed warmed themselves under the log-built picnic shelter in the park, they took inventory of all they had brought. Both felt grateful to the park ranger who was clearing fallen branches and burning them next to the shelter. Jeed commented how they could use this fire for the final ritual rather than having to build one themselves from the firewood Chris had ferried down from Seattle. The Wyrd at work. All of nature seemed to be cooperating in this event.

Josh and Paul meandered around the grounds, examining the vacant picnic area, smelling the pine scent of the giant firs. Up here the wind did not howl, the thick tree growth protecting them from its whim while the valley served to swaddle the park from extremes in weather. Jeed decided it was time to prepare for the hike up the mountain.

"Chris, do you want to take everything on your back, or do you want to leave some of this load here for the final ritual?"

"Well, I don't want to take a chance on anything being taken. I don't mind carrying it all."

Paul peeked around a wall of the shelter and asked if there was anything he could do to help. Jeed had retrieved a second pack from the jeep, but felt embarrassed at asking another man to carry his own burden. Typical. "No, I think we have everything ready," Jeed said. "Let's begin. The trail is this way."

As Jeed led the troupe into the forest, he fumbled with the second pack. Paul, following behind, skipped up beside him, put a hand on his godfather's shoulder and grabbed the strap of the second pack. Paul said nothing, but Jeed noticed the smile on his face and realized that Paul had noted his godfather's false pride. Blushing with regret, Jeed let go of the pack and smiled a thank you for Paul's thoughtfulness. As the trail reached upward, leaving the stand of trees behind, sogginess replaced carpeted ground. In some spots, puddles covered the trail completely, requiring mini-detours up rugged banks. To their left, steep terrain rose quickly to the Gorge plateaus. To the right, cliffs and even steeper descending slopes displayed rock slides dotted with hemlocks grasping tenaciously for survival. Pristine air contrasted with muddy trail. Pretending to be part mountain goat, Jeed led the crew across rock faces, hoping no one would slip or fall. He had worn his favorite hiking boots, which he considered one of the man-made wonders of the footwear world. But Josh had worn sneakers. Jeed knew the lad had been instructed to bring gear for hiking. Did he think they were going to hike in city parks? Both Chris and Paul had prepared themselves for this part of the hike.

A half-mile up the trail, Chris and Josh began to straggle behind. Paul and Jeed pulled up to wait, both of them breathing hard from the climb. After the two stragglers caught their breath, Jeed motioned Chris and Paul to take the lead, figuring they would set a better pace. As Josh edged by, Jeed gave him a pat on the shoulder. Already Josh did not look well. With growing concern, Jeed watched as Josh's sneakers kept slipping in the mud, his every step taking the effort of two normal steps. Rather than say anything or intervene, Jeed let Josh learn his lesson: never take nature for granted. Josh's Scouting days had surely made him understand the meaning of "Be Prepared." Obviously he had not prepared himself for this part of the initiation as his mom had instructed. How would he handle the rest of the climb? That remained to be seen.

As Paul and Chris continued to take detours around mud holes and puddles, Josh simply tromped through them. He was becoming a zombie. Mud oozed from under his sneakers as he slapped one foot in front of the other. Jeed felt sorry for him, but couldn't help laughing to himself. Josh looked so pathetic. They finally reached a clearing along the trail where the power lines climbed up the mountain on their journey toward Portland. Like monstrous mythological creatures made of steel, the towers held up the high-tension wires as if they were about to throw them. The surrounding landscape had been mown down to keep the wires from causing forest fires and to allow repair crews easier access. Benches made of logs invited the crew of hapless hikers to sit for a while. The clear view down to the river was both breathtaking and disgusting at the same time, man's wonder starkly contrasting with nature's wonder. If one ignored the spider web of cables zooming down the slopes, one could easily get lost in the grandeur of wetlands below, which snuggled next to the mighty Columbia. Flocks of white swans flapped their way to one of the bird sanctuaries while clouds rolled through the Gorge. Far in the distance stood Bonneville Dam, the concrete heart that pumped the millions of watts of electricity through the cabled veins overhead. Even the might of the Columbia could not escape the taming, the dominance of man.

"Is everyone rested?" Jeed asked, wanting to continue the journey so as not to be caught by early darkness. A few groans sounded as they resurrected themselves and continued the trek. Chris relieved Paul of the added burden he had volunteered for, and Paul was thankful. Jeed said nothing, knowing well enough to accept their generosity. The forest, turning the trail once again into an obstacle course of water hazards and windfall, swallowed each man as he left the ribbon of clear cut. As they trudged to a higher elevation, the rain finally stopped, and the trail became carpeted with fir needles and vegetation once again. Steeper and steeper the footpath angled until the men found themselves skirting the clouds. Even Jeed's feet began to complain, his breathing labored. *Time to bring in reserve energy*, he said to himself. With that, he moved his mind beyond ordinary reality, entering into oneness with the forest, the air, and the misty clouds dancing around him. His thoughts moved away from any sense of struggle, pain, or encroaching exhaustion. In this state of oneness, he lost the edges of who he was and what nature wasn't. The energy of the living world around him started to fill him with its cornucopia of life force, or what the Chinese call *chi*. Each step became a dance in a trance of bliss.

"Jeed, I can't go on," gasped Josh. "I don't have any energy left."

"We only have another half-mile to go." Jeed tried to encourage him.

"I can't," he announced bent over like a broken sapling. "I don't have any energy left in my body." There they stood for a while. After a few minutes, Chris hiked down to join the two.

"Are you OK, Josh?" asked Dad, concerned at the look on his son's face.

"No, I'm not," he choked out, near tears. "I can't go on. I'm exhausted." Chris looked over at Jeed who looked back with a half smile. As Paul now joined the group, Jeed knew it was time for the next step. Gently he turned the spent Josh to face him. The effort was like moving a puppet. A simple push and he would have gone over the edge of the nearby cliff like a discarded toy, resisting nothing, not even death.

"Josh, I know you feel like you have nothing left in you, but it is time for you to become aware of another kind of energy. You don't just have energy in your body. Energy is all around you. Have you noticed the way I have been breathing for the last quarter-mile?"

"No. I haven't noticed anything except how tired and sore I am."

"This breathing I use is called pranic breathing. It's a technique used by ancient cultures to access this surrounding energy. I would like you to try this. You willing to give it a try?" Still gasping for air, Josh nodded yes. "Close your eyes and begin to breathe deeply. Don't just breathe in air. See the air as energy, feel the air as energy, imagine the air as nothing but energy. Now let me know when you see this energy." Closing his eyes, Josh began to breathe deeply. While a youngster in junior high, the forward-thinking school had taught meditation techniques to many of the kids whose parents had given permission. Focusing on himself, Josh used this knowledge to calm himself and to visualize the air as energy. Chris watched with interest as his son began to breathe in slow deliberate breaths. After about a minute of breathing, Josh opened his eyes. "I can imagine the air having energy, but I don't feel anything. I don't think it's working."

"Give it some time," said Jeed. "As we continue, keep breathing the way you are now. Feel the air; thank the air each time it enters your lungs. Acknowledge the air as it gives energy to your body. Then thank the air again as it leaves your body, carrying away the tiredness. Energy is all around you. It's yours for the asking. Just become constantly aware of the air and the rest will follow. Just try it. Be sure to think about each and every breath. Concentrate on each and every breath. Thank each and every breath."

Chris watched intently as all this went on. As Josh closed his eyes again and continued his deep breathing, Chris asked in a comic-hurtful way, "How come you never showed me that?"

"You never asked," answered Jeed with a wink. As they started back up the trail, Paul took the lead with Jeed following. Chris brought up the rear to keep an eye on Josh. As they pursued their ascent into the clouds, Jeed could hear Josh breathing. *Good*, he said to himself, then turned to see Chris taking in deep breaths as well. He had to smile, thinking that any nearby hikers would swear a herd of snorting llamas must be climbing the mountain. As they trudged on, Josh commented once more how he thought that Jeed's exercise wasn't working. However, he kept putting one foot in front of the other, continuing his breathing. No one said anything for quite a while. Sometimes Jeed would just listen to the wind in the trees, focusing on his oneness with the wind itself, sometimes listening to the breathing of Josh and Chris. All sounded harmonious to him.

The upper reaches of the climb greeted the line of snorting llamas with the waltzing of clouds, the mist pleasantly resting on their faces, cooling the heat of exertion. In the distance, Jeed began to hear the rumble of distant water. He smiled as the trail began to level off. Josh would make it after all. Step after rhythmic step slowly brought them close to their destination. The world of trees turned into a world of enchantment. Mosses hung from limbs like lacy veils on the arms of ladies. Billows of mist rose from the ravine below like ghost riders galloping up the mountainside. Interesting, thought Jeed, how the clouds now seemed to mimic the dancing wind at Beacon Rock, as if taking on a life of their own. Like a curtain going up on stage, the clouds revealed a special welcome for the next act of ritual.

"Wow!" bellowed Chris as he gawked at the raging creek below. The rain had filled the creek to overflowing. Huge cascades of foaming white water thundered down the ravine.

"Wait till you see what's ahead," yelled Jeed. As they turned the bend, journey's end lay before them. Two hundred yards away thundered Rodney Falls. Unlike other falls in the area, it spilled off the plateau above into a large chamber carved into the rock, which

155

magnified the sound like the inside of a drum. The falls disappeared into the rock wall, exploding through the bottom opening with sprays of white mist, creating an illusion of boiling steam materializing out of solid rock. As the crew neared, they could see the definition of the hollow chamber a bit better, the growl from its gaping mouth deafening. Jeed turned to see Josh's eyes widening.

"Thank God," muttered the young initiate, forgetting his exhaustion. Jeed had to smile at the defeated youngster's previous insistence that he had no energy and could not go on. He seemed not to have noticed that the breathing "hadn't worked."

Paul stopped to get a panoramic view of the watery world they had entered: clouds, mist, waterfall, and creek, thundering with life. Jeed leaned close to Paul's ear and spoke above the noise a passage from Scripture: "For an angel came down upon the waters, and the waters were stirred." Never had Jeed seen the cauldron of waterfall and creek so magnificent as on this day. The creek had never been so alive and full. Normally, visitors can reach the spillway from the approaching ledge. Steel railings had been erected over the years, allowing sightseers to lean over the edge and gaze into the chamber at what the locals called the Pool of the Winds. But not today. Water poured over the approaching ledge, flooding the path to the chamber. Jeed had hoped to show the guys how he could penetrate the mist and disappear into the chamber for a private swim. But today, spray spewed twenty or thirty feet straight out from the stone cliffs. So instead, everyone sat on an aging cedar bench flanking the cliff. No one said a word, giving their bodies a much-needed rest while their eyes feasted on the scene before them. Jeed gave thanks that no others had climbed to the site.

After several minutes of absorbing the wonder, Chris broke the silence. "Wow! This was worth it." Josh sat transfixed, overwhelmed by all his eyes, ears, and starving body were telling him. Paul got up to examine the waterfall and the large pool. He knew the role he was designated to play here. The planning and plotting of the previous months were in his hands. The rain subsided in cooperation, as the wind had on top of Beacon Rock.

"Chris," shouted Jeed, "can you hand me that pack you carried up for me?"

"Sure. Time we begin?"

"Yeah. I'll go yell at Paul to come over here." Sound filled the entire ravine so completely that any conversation other than shouting drowned in the thunder of water. After retrieving Paul, Jeed opened the knapsack and extracted a wooden bowl and three towels.

"I don't have to go into that water, do I?" whined Josh, still hanging onto his fear of having to strip naked.

"Just watch and listen," shouted Jeed. "We'll tell you what's next." A part of Jeed felt sorry for Josh, yet another part was a bit annoyed.

Chris opened his pack and took out a small drum about the diameter of a small frying pan. On the skin of the drum he had painted in red and black the Northwest Native design of a salmon. Chris loved the salmon as a totem. He respected it not only as a fisherman but also as a student of Northwest history and lore. "I need someone to play the drum for me." Drumming not being Jeed's forte, he pointed at Paul. The three then stood in front of Josh, who started to stand also.

"No, you just sit there," commanded Jeed. "I'd like you to take off your shoes and socks, though, and then we'll begin." Josh hesitated a moment, caught up in his own imagination of what was going to transpire. Slowly he peeled off his soggy sneakers and soaked socks. Jeed nodded to Chris to begin. Chris in turn asked Paul to begin the drumbeat.

"Whatever feels right to you. Let the drum reflect who you are at this moment." Paul considered how the drum should sing what he felt. Grasping the drumstick, he paused in midair. Then slowly the voice of the drum joined that of the waterfall, its tenor voice rising above the choir of grumbling rumble that shook the ground beneath their feet. About a minute into the drumming, Chris began once again his spirit-calling song, tenor on tenor in harmony with the waterfall of many voices. The song sounded sweeter than ever. Over and over, Chris sang out the song, tears and all. When he had finished, the drum continued to sing its aria, never stopping, ever reminding the men of the symphony of life around them. The moment intoxicated them. The drudgery of the strenuous hike dropped away like a useless raincoat. Sacred space opened before them once again.

Jeed picked up the chestnut bowl. He had spied the large salad bowl at a garage sale and knew right away his weeks of scouting garage sales had paid off. As the drum continued its beat, Jeed walked over to the Pool of the Winds, the exploding spray coating him in wetness. With deliberate solemnity he dipped the bowl into the icy pool, stood up, holding the bowl at eye level, and stepped methodically toward Josh. Lifting the bowl heavenward, he prayed aloud, "I ask the spirit of the waters to bless this bowl I hold in my hands. May we be worthy as men to be cleansed by the pure water it holds. I breathe my own life into this water as a sign of the oneness of my spirit with that of the water." Then, holding the bowl at chest level, he took a deep breath and slowly let out a hiss of breath upon the water. Three times he did this to symbolize the three balancing forces of life: the masculine, the feminine, and the androgynous.

Josh watched half curious and half dazed as if a spell had come upon him. Jeed then passed the bowl to Chris and then to Paul, asking each to breathe upon the water. With simple humility, Jeed placed the bowl at Josh's feet and knelt on the ground in front of him. Picking up Josh's left foot and holding it over the water, he began to scoop handfuls of water and trickle it down the foot. Josh sucked in air, surprised by the iciness, but said nothing, trying to hide his discomfort.

"Josh, I kneel here before you as a servant would kneel before a Teacher. This is to let you know we must all be servants to one another as men. It is also to let you know how we must learn to receive from one another. If we allow ourselves to receive from one another, then we also can serve as teachers to one another. You have seen me as a teacher and as a father figure for years, calling me your other-father. You must no longer see me as a father figure but as an equal. If you ever have need of me, then you have only to ask of me as an equal. It is important for you to realize how you are also a teacher to me as I have been to you. From this day forward, we walk together as men.

"May this water serve as a reminder for you to have purity of purpose as you walk your path in life. Feel the difference within you as I wash your foot as opposed to how you feel when you wash your own foot. Does it not change you when another man is willing to help you, be of service to you? Remember this feeling as you continue to help others." As Jeed spoke, he continued to pour water over the warm foot. Quietly he retrieved a towel and began to dry the foot, taking time to accentuate the ways of a servant. Josh felt uncomfortable and didn't know why. Was Jeed being pretentious? Was this a big deal? Or was it embarrassingly corny? Josh could not unravel his mixed emotions.

Upon finishing, Jeed stood once again and prayed, "I return this water to the earth. It has touched not only my life but Josh's life. May our lives be brought together forever as men through this ritual of water." With continued solemnity, he walked alongside the pool, and with a forceful toss threw the water into a thousand droplets, which merged with the white foam plunging down the cliffs. Ceremoniously he passed the bowl on to Chris.

After retrieving water from the pool with some difficulty, Chris began his prayer over the water, Josh's eyes traveling up and down the full figure of his father. But was this his father? What were these grown men trying to convey to him? Brotherhood? Benediction? Or mystery beyond understanding?

"Josh, you and I have traveled together through this life in a special way." Chris's words hit Josh, forcing his eyes down to the freshly washed foot. "Like Jeed said, as your father I have been your guide and your teacher, but you have also been mine. I was there when you were born. It was from a watery womb you were born. And once again, you are born to the world in a new way through water. I watch how the waterfall sweeps through the forest, cleaning not only the valley floor but also the air with its spray. The rains fall and cleanse all they touch. You are a part of the Earth as we all are part of the Earth. As men, we have the power to touch one another as rain touches the earth. I acknowledge this power in you. I ask you to see it in yourself as I now wash you with this water."

As Chris knelt to begin the ritual washing of Josh's other foot, his throat swelled with emotion. Jeed's eyes began to turn red. *If only I had been given such a father as this*, he said to himself. As Chris began trickling the water down Josh's foot, old memories haunted Jeed. What contrast were Chris's words to the words Jeed had heard so often from his own father: "If I had wanted to send a fool, I would have done it myself." Was his witnessing Chris's words a sign that the world truly was changing?

"Let this serve as a sign that I fully accept you as a man," Chris continued, the words catching in his throat. "I will continue to help you as a father would. But no longer will I assume I can help you just because I have been your father. No longer will I tell you to do things, but will ask you, invite you. From this day forward, you have the power over when and how I can help you. Know that you can ask of me as any other man would ask of me. Know that I will not interfere in your life; I will not move into your life unless invited. But also know that I shall ask of you as I would any other man. You, too, have the strength and the power to help me. I am proud to have you as my son, and even prouder to call you a man."

As Chris dried Josh's foot, Josh's eyes stared fixed on the ground, his ears growing bright red. But not from embarrassment. His heart overflowed. And so did his eyes. No longer could he contain the mixture of emotions. A swarm of teardrops splashed down on his parka. Not a muscle moved, not even to breathe. If he had been a balloon, the slightest touch would have burst him. Chris stood, looking for a place to leave the towel. As Jeed took it from him, he could see both the pain and the joy on his friend's face. Chris may have lost his youngest boy, but he had lovingly given the world a special man. This remarkable father's proud smile acknowledged the truth of his words: He had received into his life not just a man, but a loving man who would be his support and strength through his remaining years, just the way Chris had supported and helped Josh through his boyhood. Such a paradox that our children end up caring for us in old age the way we care for them in infancy.

The drumbeat grew stronger as Chris carried the bowl of water back to the volcano of spray. Paul was getting ready for his turn. After a slightly clumsy exchange with the drum and the bowl, Chris continued the thumping, closing his eyes while letting his heart speak through the heartbeat of the drum. Paul returned with the wooden bowl full once again. He stood before Josh and waited. After a pause, he leaned over to Jeed and asked, "Can I say whatever I want, or should I try and say some kind of prayer?"

Jeed smiled at his sincerity and replied, "Say whatever you want."

Paul continued standing before his brother for a few moments while gathering his thoughts. "We are all part of the river we call Life, Josh. And I'll explain that later. I want you to know how proud I am to be your brother. As I put your feet into this water, I want you to understand that from this day forward my feet will always be in the water with yours, also. For the rest of our days, we will dangle our feet together in the river. And I'll explain that, too." Paul began to place the bowl beneath Josh's feet. But unlike Chris and Jeed, he knew he was to do something different. Initiation rituals need to have a memorable part to them, something to shock the body but not to harm it. The body has a memory of its own and can serve to keep a ritual event long remembered. Paul had purposely filled the bowl to the brim, soaking his pant legs while trying carefully to carry it back to the ritual space. As Paul placed the bowl beneath his brother's feet, some of the water began to spill, giving the appearance of clumsiness. While pretending to shake the cold water from his hands, he immediately grabbed Josh's two feet and plunged them fully into the water. Josh's backbone stiffened like an icicle as he let out a loud "Uhhhhhhh!" Snow-melt cold, the water burned instead of cooled. As Paul continued speaking, he forced the feet in place. "Let this be a sign of our brotherhood as men." Josh's eyes bulged as his feet began to ache. "Know that I accept you and respect you as a man. As your brother, I will be at your side should you ever need me. As a man, I know that I can depend on you should I ever need help." Josh began inhaling and exhaling in short, choppy gasps as Paul refused to let his feet out of the water. A giggle gurgled up from Paul. "I have something I would like to give you so that you understand this as I understand it." As Paul released Josh's feet, he yanked them from the water, and exhaled a sigh of relief.

Paul retrieved a small package he had carefully wrapped in plastic. He lay the gift beside the bowl as his attention turned to drying his younger brother's feet. "This is a book, a very special book. It changed my life." After wiping off the last of the icy drops, Paul continued, "The name of this book is *Siddhartha*. It was written by a guy named Hermann Hesse. It's a story about two friends and the Ganges River. Before I read this book, I felt disconnected from my own spirituality. I hope what this book had to say to me will be as revealing to you. I hope you will be able to have a similar experience as I had.

"The river is like humanity, like people. Everybody is a part of the river, moving and flowing with life, and around life. Every person in our lives is somehow a part of this river, but the river is also a part of the humongous whole that is the totality of all the rivers in the world flowing into the sea. From above, we can see how all rivers are connected to the ocean. That's how I feel about my own spirituality. I'm just a part of one river flowing into the ocean.

"You going through this ritual, this initiation, has made you the beginning of a small river of manhood. Like this creek here beside us. You have joined the river of manhood that is a part of life. It is my hope you will always be a part of my life and that our lives will peacefully flow together. When we become old men, it is my hope that we will be able to dangle our feet together in the river of life, telling stories like the one happening here today. Here," he said as he handed the wrapped paperback to Josh, who accepted it without a word.

Paul may have been just out of high school, but somehow he sounded like the wisest man there. Jeed stood speechless, witnessing the scene of the two brothers. Josh finally spoke as he quickly flipped through the pages of the book. "It may take me a while to get through it, but I will keep it always. Thanks, Paul."

"Sure" was all Paul said, knowing that Josh would fully understand once he had read the story of Govinda and Siddhartha. As Paul carried the bowl over to the creek's edge to return it to its journey to the river below, Jeed signaled Chris to cease the drumming and instructed Josh to put on his shoes and socks. Josh wrung his socks out like a wet dishrag before putting them on his numb feet. One Paul returned, Jeed took the bowl one more time and walked to the waterfall. This time, he climbed onto the steel railing and edged himself to the foaming waters surging from the chamber. Trying unsuccessfully not to get caught in the spray, he stretched out and caught enough water to clean out the bowl, and then filled it for the last time. After squirming his way back along the railing, he returned to the circle of men.

Holding the bowl high in the air, Jeed prayed one more time: "I give thanks for these waters of life. May we remember this day as we, like the river, continue our journey to wholeness. As each of us drinks from this common bowl, we acknowledge our oneness with nature, our oneness with the spirit realm, and our oneness with one another." Then, bringing the bowl to his lips, he sipped of the fresh, cold water and passed the bowl to Chris. Each took a drink, returning the bowl to Jeed. "I return this water that has touched our lips, that has touched our lives, and return it to nature, from whence it came. As it continues on its journey, we continue on ours — together, as men, as brothers." With one last fling he tossed the water into the spray cascading down the cliff and set the bowl upon the ground.

"Chris, would you close with your spirit song once more?" As Chris began his chant, he reached his arms around Jeed and Josh, who in turn put their arms around Paul. There they stood, the four of them in the midst of natural wonder, feeling like the gods of ages past. No sooner had the chant begun than it began to rain once again. Chris's voice sounded at home with all the voices of the waters: rain, waterfall, spray, and wind-driven clouds. Life was meant to feel this good. The song lines were like knitting needles that had knit their souls together, with the spirits of the waters having been their witnesses. None wanted to leave. None wanted to let the others go.

They felt more than their humanity with one another. They felt their sacredness.

Chapter Eleven

RITUAL BY FIRE

*I*n silence, all four men merged back into the forest. Even though Jeed had not requested silence, as before, words had no place. What had happened at the falls left all in a state of reverie. Unlike Josh's struggle up the trail, he took the lead down, his footsteps no longer exhibiting his earlier pathetic condition. Now his gait was alive. Chris, however, struggled behind, his old legs complaining about the long day.

Paul walked deep in thought, as if alone. He remembered feeling similarly years ago, while up at Priest Lake after a Fourth of July weekend. Chris, Josh, Paul, and Uncle Frank had decided the four of them should go camping — just the guys. Jeed had chosen to pursue his favorite pastime in the high Selkirks: searching for highly prized huckleberries. All the relatives had left, and with them the hubbub of activity surrounding the holiday weekend: a sumptuous barbecue, canoe trips for the youngsters, fly fishing the rivers with cousins, water skiing for the more athletic, and a plethora of board games and word games to accentuate the evenings. Time to get away and have some fun — guy fun. And off the four of them embarked in the sixteen-foot Bayliner to Bartoo Island in the middle of Priest Lake. But everyone called the island Bare Toe, it being anything but bare.

Paul loved Bare Toe because of its thick forest and calm waters on the south side. No other island in the large lake possessed such wide and sandy beaches. The wind-shadow effect made it one of the more popular spots for launching on water skis. That evening found the island free of vacationers and water skiers. Twilight had lasted until after ten on that clear summer night. Paul remembered how magical their arrival had been as they drifted into shore after cutting the engine in the shallows.

Uncle Frank jumped from the bow to pull the boat onto the beach, then slammed the anchor into the pearl-rice sand. Chris searched for the perfect spot to pitch tents, for he usually had to sleep by himself — a fair distance from the others. His snoring was legendary. Like his father, Paul usually found himself exiled to a private tent as well. Sleeping in the same tent with him was like sleeping with a giant Mexican jumping bean in a sleeping bag. No matter how big the tent, Paul would manage to travel the entire expanse by morning.

With tents pitched, Uncle Frank decided it was time to go skinny-dipping. Unfortunately, Frank had forgotten that Bare Toe had one of the largest colonies of red ants imaginable. While taking off his clothes in exactly the wrong spot, carefully folding each removed garment, a swarm of ants managed to find his feet. After folding his undershorts, he realized that the little beasties had crawled up to his thighs, and were rising rapidly into forbidden territory. With a scream that sounded like half war whoop and half damsel in distress, Frank tried brushing off the little critters as if they were bread crumbs on a dirty table. Of course that only allowed the little red warriors to attack his hands. Like some scene out of an Alfred Hitchcock movie, Frank sprinted for the lake covered in ants, the fiery sunset accentuating his measles-like appearance as he took a flying leap into the water.

Paul's and Chris's laughter echoed across the glassy lake from shore to shore. Twelve-year-old Josh feared Uncle Frank might die;

at least it sounded as if he were dying as he had plunged into water. After ample time submerged, Uncle Frank finally broke the surface. "Come on in; the water's great," he yelled in celebratory tones, as if nothing had happened. Paul was imagining little red bodies backstroking for shore. No way he was going in.

"Why not?" Chris sang out. In less than a minute, another naked body plunged into the welcoming waters. Not to be left out, Paul joined in with a cannonball entry — better to discourage any tiny red floaters. Josh stood on the shore wishing he could join in. Chris tried to tease young Josh into the water after a couple of water fights with Frank and Paul. "The water's really nice after you get in."

"I didn't bring no swimming suit," Josh protested. "Someone might see me." Ever the modest wonder. After several attempts to convince Josh that no one could see anything at this distance from the mainland, he finally stepped behind a tent and removed his clothing in a manner that made one wonder if he were removing dried paint. With his head constantly rotating, looking for spies, he tiptoed through the grainy sand and stopped abruptly as his feet touched the water. "It's freezing!" he yelled, so loud that the word "freezing" bounced back and forth across the quiet lake.

"No it's not," Chris growled. "Just get in and you'll be fine." Eventually the four of them were swimming like playful otters. The dusk sky glowed even redder, silhouetting the forest-covered mountains. Stars began to twinkle through. This was Shangri-La, and they had it all to themselves.

Paul helped Chris gather wood for a fire while Uncle Frank and Josh began scooping up sand for the building of the traditional sand pyramid. Frank loved building sand pyramids. Not so much because they looked beautiful. He just loved the way they caved in when the boys jumped into the middle of them. The sturdy nature of Bare Toe's grainy, beadlike sand made for the best sand pyramids.

In short order, Paul and Chris had a roaring fire going to warm their goose-bumped bodies. More and more driftwood fed the fire. This was going to be an all-nighter. They told ghost stories as the logs turned red with coals. Uncle Frank took a couple of driftwood sticks and began thumping on one of the ember-laden logs. Showers of sparks rose into the night air. Like a native of the night, he began to chant, sending even more sparks into the darkness. Chris joined in. Paul hunted for sticks at the edge of the woods so he and Josh could accompany them. There the four of them were, pounding their drumsticks into the fire, singing make-believe "Indian" babble with clouds of sparks rising above them like fire spirits. The ambience turned mystical, eye-fixing magical. The fire spirits danced before them like belly dancers while their voices sang out made-up war chants. Paul's soul stirred as he listened to his father and his uncle chant, spellbound by the mystery of the fire and its dancing sparks, mystery he had never understood until this moment, as he walked down the Hamilton Mountain trail. There is something unknown and deep within a man, something primitive, eons old. Something that only awakens in nature, and once awakened, it desires song and dance with the spirits of nature.

The most memorable event of that night at Bare Toe, however, was not the magic and the mystery. It was something equally strong within a man: foolishness. Paul smiled as he reconstructed the scene in his mind. The coals in the fire had faded to the point where no more showers of sparks could be beaten out. So Chris decided they should clean up the entire south beach of its Fourth of July litter. They gathered all the burnable litter and dumped it into the fire pit, resurrecting the fire one more time. The many vacationers had left behind paper, plastic, spent fireworks tubes, and boxes of all kinds. To the common bystander, the hill of trash on the growing fire might have seemed startling. Chris fanned the fire until the flames rose to consume the refuse, the hard cardboard tubing, and the many boxes. As the fire grew hotter, a dud firecracker exploded into life, scaring Josh. They all laughed. But the laughter died immediately when, without warning, bottle rockets spewed skyward from out of the flames. Exploding firecrackers scattered burning debris everywhere, shattering the still night with staccato booms. All of a sudden, they found themselves in a war zone where an invisible enemy had detonated an ammo dump. More blasts filled the air. Everyone ran for the lake as whistlers screamed in all directions into the night. One whistler screamed right into the forest, lodging itself in a tree where it spun madly, sending out sparks into dry pine needles.

"Quick!" yelled Chris. "Get some water." They were about to set the whole of Bare Toe Island ablaze. Frank crawled into the boat searching for a bucket. All he could find was a small bailing bucket. He dipped it into the lake and ran to the tree. Tossing the water as high as he could, he managed only to wet the lower limbs. The higher branch began to smolder. Still more firecrackers exploded from the fire pit. Another whistler shot off into the forest. No one dared approach the volcano of sparks. Now cherry bombs began exploding, sending everything in the pit a thousand directions, but also managing to blow out the fire. Only by dumb luck did nothing hit the tents. The guys slowly assembled around the vacant fire pit, as the one tree smoldered even more. Like escaped convicts staring at a dead body, they gawked at the few remains of dying coals, then gawked at one another.

"What are we going to do?" asked Paul. "Should we go get some help?"

"No," said Chris, trying to maintain a calm voice. "I think we'll be OK. I'll sleep out here near the tree so I can tell if it catches fire. If it does, we'll leave in the boat and go get help." They all slept cautiously that night. Chris kept one eye on the smoldering tree branch the whole night long while the rest slept in their tents. The fire spirits no longer seemed so magical, so enticing, so friendly. When man was given fire, he was given more than a great gift. He also was given a great responsibility.

Paul never forgot that night. After that, they visited Bare Toe Island every year, traditionally checking out the old tree, retelling the story to any who would listen. The last time Bare Toe had been visited, and the last time the story had been told was when all the guys, including Jeed, went together to build a pyramid of cement and pearly sand on its rocky point. This was their memorial to Uncle Frank, who had committed suicide earlier that year. The pyramid stands to this day among the granite rocks of Bare Toe's point. A brass plate is embedded in the west side of the pyramid, facing the setting sun. On it is inscribed, "To Frank. Brother, uncle, and friend. Pee-wee, are you sure?" That last summer spent with Frank, he had bombarded everyone with Pee-wee Herman jokes. He had never missed a Pee-wee Herman special, nor failed to remember a Pee-wee Herman story. Whenever he questioned anything, he used an often-repeated quote from *Pee-wee's Playhouse*: "Pee-wee, are you sure?" The brass plaque served as a testimonial to Frank's joy, his child-hearted ways, as well as a testimony to the hole his absence had left in their hearts.

But nothing could be taken away from that night when the fire spirits had danced in the sparks above the fire pit. Paul knew the four of them had felt as one, each soul a spark from a common fire of love. Tragic how Uncle Frank's spark had gone out. But his absence took nothing away from the mysterious fire Paul felt inside himself, a fire that could not be dampened, a fire growing in Paul as he silently followed Josh back down the trail to the final ritual. A ritual by fire.

Chris had to rest with increasing frequency. His legs were prone to cramping once his body reached exhaustion. His need for water also increased, causing him to fall farther and farther behind. Toward the final stretch of the trail, Josh finally noticed his dad had fallen out of sight. He stopped, collecting Jeed and Paul, waiting for their straggler to catch up. Ironically, they waited in the same spot where Josh himself had sworn he could go no farther. Now, chattering away like a chipmunk, spirited and fresh, he half joked, "Wow, Dad. We've been waiting half an hour for you to catch up. You must be outta shape. Gettin' kind of old." He grinned at the others as Chris sat and massaged his calves to keep them from cramping more.

"Yeah, I guess," he grimaced. A part of Jeed bristled at watching this, feeling the need to remind Josh that this was an initiation rite.

"Josh," Jeed said. "It's time you understand, now that you are a man, that men are meant to honor one another, uphold one another, not make fun of one another or belittle one another. The days of put-downs should be left for your boyish friends. You are now at a time in your life when you have the power to change, to influence all that is around you. A man must choose whether he is a victim of life or a supporter of life. You can choose to influence all of life around you rather than be influenced by it. There is a responsibility that comes with this power. And that responsibility includes the capacity to know when another man is in need of help or understanding or compassion. Your father has endured the strain of the hike for your benefit. Yet you return his caring and his effort with a put-down. I know you are only joking, but it is time for you to realize that you don't have to be a part of such banter, such shaming. This has become a national pastime in our country. Frankly, it injures all men. It reflects the lack of tolerance and compassion in our society as a whole. Remember how you feel when you are shamed. Older men are to be respected for their wisdom, for surviving all that has tried to weaken them, for being able to teach those who are younger, less wise. Their days of wisdom can be for you a guiding light. Rather than showing your own strength by pointing out another's weakness, you would find far greater reward in lifting up others with your strength, lending a helping hand."

A strained silence fell across Josh. It was he who now felt shame, making him aware how uncomfortable its weight. His face flushed as he looked over at his dad. Chris gave no indication one way or the other how he felt about Jeed's reproach. Paul scratched his nose as he took in the whole scene.

"Dad, would it help if I carried your pack for you?" asked Josh. A smile sneaked across Chris's face. The thoughtfulness of his young son felt like a healing balm.

"Maybe for a little while. I can handle it on flatter ground."

As Josh received the pack and slung it over his free shoulder, a calm filled him. What a difference, he realized, to joke about a man's weakness as opposed to lifting up a man in his hour of weakness. What a difference to use strength as a benefit rather than to use witty words as a weapon. He would never forget this lesson. A half-mile later, as all rested silently for the final time, not far from the trailhead, Chris volunteered to carry his pack the rest of the way. Josh insisted it wasn't heavy. Jeed smiled, for the two packs he himself had lugged back down were burdening him noticeably by this time. Good to see such strength from this young man, even while Jeed felt his own growing weakness.

As the four emerged from the forest and into the picnic area, they could see that the ranger's fire had consumed most of the branches and logs, leaving only blue flames and red-hot coals hissing in the spitting rain. Perfect for what they needed. The sun was beginning to hide on this shortest day of the year. Dusk gave the park a sleepy feel. The wind no longer blew; the tall firs drooped in the quiet, giants in a land of enchantment, ready to doze off. The glowing fire beckoned with its warmth. All but Chris accepted. The electricity of feeling so alive traveled through them as they stared at the coals, steam rising from their wet trousers. The fallen limbs had filled the park with the perfume of Christmas. Wet moss yielded a musty odor not unlike mistletoe. Uncommon joy mesmerized them as merry blue and orange flames danced in and out of embers.

Chris appeared from the log shelter, carrying a small bag slung over his shoulder. In the shadows he could have been mistaken for some elfin figure as he scurried over to the fire on his toes, half skipping, half dancing. A twinkle lit his eyes and a warm grin his face. "I'm ready." He wondered why the rest hadn't budged a whisker.

"Why don't we all sit," suggested Jeed in a quiet voice. Commandeered rocks and leftover logs served as stools as they huddled near the fire. As before, Chris opened the ritual with his spirit-calling song, made more rich by its echoing among trees. Steam rose from Josh's sneakers to the point where Jeed wondered what was steam and what was smoke. Josh's eyes stared transfixed at the coals. Not an eyelid moved. What a contrast from the trail, where Chris had been dragging his butt while the rest nearly bounded down the last section of the trail. But now Chris had transformed into Saint Nick, awake and jovial, while the other three looked like they might keel over into the fire with the touch of a feather. What had changed? Apparently, this was the moment Chris had been waiting for all day.

"Josh?" prompted Jeed. The lad still hadn't done anything but breathe, and barely that.

"Yeah?" he mouthed, without moving his lips.

"Do you have your journal with you?" Paul now peered at his statuelike brother, clouds of steam rising off him in the cool of the evening.

"Yeah," his voice said, drifting up from his throat.

"Would you get it, please?"

Without a word, the statue slowly came to life and trundled over to the shed. As he returned, wisps of steam continued trailing from his clothing. He sat in the same exact spot in the same exact pose as before, the journal tucked between his forearm and coat.

"I'd like you to open your journal one more time and read us the part about Josh-the-boy."

Stiff hands fumbled for the right page. Stoically, he read once again the words composed on the train. But the sentences only seemed to be words with no meaning attached to them. Who was this boy he was reading about? Did he ever exist? Josh was having a difficult time even recognizing the words. It was as if he were in another world where he didn't even know who Josh was. Life around him didn't seem like life. More like a stage with people moving through their parts. The stage hands, invisible as they were, couldn't be recognized either. Nothing was recognizable. Nothing was real. He had never felt like this before. Was this what Jeed had been trying to tell him? What Native American cultures believed? That the "real" world truthfully rests within our dreams, whereas what we call reality is in fact an illusion? The colors in the fire shifted. The flames had become small flickering rainbows. Josh's emotions moved beyond feeling into what can only be described as tangibility. It was as if he could touch his emotions. But he didn't dare to or wish to touch them. They might come to life. He wasn't sure he should open that door. It might never be closed again. For now, his emotions had to remain invisible like the stagehands of the imaginary stage. Emotions had always betrayed the boy. They had made him a sissy among would-be friends. They had been mocked in the presence of grown-ups. They had betrayed him at the most inappropriate times, when he hadn't wanted anyone to know of the storms within his heart. As he came to the last sentence of this section of his journal, he recalled nothing of what he had just read.

"OK, Josh. I would like you to tear the page from your journal and throw it into the fire."

"This page, or all the pages I wrote on?"

"Only the page about the boy."

A shocked look crept across Josh's face. Mechanically, the fingernails of his left hand caught the top edge of the page and ripped down. The remnants of the page curled along the inside edge of the journal like frozen paper flames. He felt as if he had wounded his journal. How strange. *How can a journal be wounded?* he asked himself. *What is happening to me? I feel stupid.* How could he feel compassion for something lifeless like his journal? Maybe it wasn't lifeless after all. Maybe he had given it life when he wrote in it. *Weird*, he thought to himself. *The hunger must be making me hallucinate. Or maybe I'm starting to go crazy.*

Reluctantly, Josh threw the crumpled page into the red-hot coals. He watched it writhe, turning toasty, then black, as it burst into flames. He felt as if he had betrayed a friend, sending him to certain death. Gone forever.

"You are no longer a boy, Josh. You remain only a man." Jeed pronounced the words as if he were a wizard casting a spell. "From this day forward, you will leave behind the ways of the boy. You will inherit the ways of men. The boy is dead." The words stunned Josh. His mouth hung open as he fixed on the remaining ashes of the boy he had written about. Something inside drained out of his body and melted into the fire. Bare Toe Island came to his mind, the night the sparks had danced in the air. The boy who had lived inside him now joined the fire spirits, forever held in another dimension, never to return. He felt scared, not unlike how he had felt when the tree almost caught fire. Was he like the island? In threat of being consumed by fire? He tried to dismiss his feelings. *What is there to be scared of?* Wasn't it just a stupid piece of paper in a park ranger's fire pit? Once again, he felt the tangibility of his emotions. They strained to be set free, to dance with the fire spirits and the

174

spirit of the boy. But no. They couldn't be let out. Even if the boy were gone.

"I will tell you one of the secrets of manhood, Josh," said Jeed. Everyone's eyes fixed on the steaming statue of the proclaimed man as the fire illuminated the strange mask he wore. His face obviously was trying to hide something. Everyone could see that. But what was there to hide? "I and other men will share secrets with you as you progress through manhood. They will help you in your quest to become yourself, to live the life you were born to live. From this day forward, you must understand that no one — no man, no woman, no teacher, no boss, no enemy, no corporation, no government, and no army — has power over you. You are and shall continue to be your own ultimate power. No one but no one can make you do anything unless you personally will to do it. Not even God has the power to override your own free will. There is no force on this Earth that can make you do one single, solitary thing unless you yourself decide to do it. Always remember that. You even have the choice of choosing death over the power of an enemy or an army. A man has total rule over his own being. This can be a great power when used wisely, or it can be a great tragedy if used selfishly. Neither I nor your father nor your mother have any claim over you from this day forward unless you will it. You now possess the power to affect life more than life has the power to affect you. Think about my words. Hear them. Use this power wisely. You are a gifted human being. Use your gift to the fullest and you will bring blessing to all around you."

Jeed had little more to say. His role as Elder was close to completion. The boy in Josh had been killed. All that remained was the man, the son, the brother, the all-powerful spirit of the human being. Jeed knew the truth of his words. The power he had unleashed within Josh was real. Jeed had come by this knowledge in his own way years ago. A single unexpected day, a day of internal horror, had changed him forever. And he intended that Josh should know what Jeed had uncovered that terrible day. That Josh should be changed as he had been changed. If Josh took the pronouncement to his heart, he would know, feel, and always remember its truth, its power. Josh would play the game of life as a master of his own destiny rather than as a victim of unavoidable circumstances. He had been blessed greatly. And to those to whom much is given, much is expected by Heaven.

Jeed's own moment of awareness of this power came while he was finishing his final year of service in the Air Force. A mere sergeant in Air Force Intelligence, he had been stationed at the most top-secret place in the world: the National Security Agency, NSA, also known as the "Puzzle Palace." His days at Fort Meade had bored him. The Air Force had trained him for electronic spying on Communist Romania, which meant he spoke Romanian better than most Romanians spoke Romanian. Little did he know that his days of boredom, gathering intelligence on a country no one in the intelligence community much cared about, would change him irrevocably.

The Soviet Union had just invaded what was then called Czechoslovakia. In what later became known as the "Prague Spring," the might of the Soviet Army crushed the socialist experiment of Communist leader Alexandr Dubcek, sending in massive numbers of tanks and troops. Intelligence knew that Soviet troops were now massing on the Romanian border, next to Czechoslovakia. Lyndon Johnson was President, known in the intelligence community for his unpredictable political ruthlessness. Rumor had reached the Romanian intelligence office in NSA that the Soviets wanted to kill two birds with one stone by also dethroning Romanian Communist leader Nicolae Ceausescu, a rebellious thorn in the side of Soviet Russia.

Like any other day, Jeed sat at his translation station with headphones on, listening to the same boring stuff he always listened to, when all of a sudden someone from behind yanked off his headset. Turning around to chew out whoever was behind the prank, Jeed stared at a flank of higher-ups staring at him. An officer had a memorandum in his hand. "Sergeant, this is from the President," he announced in an ominous tone. "The Russians are about to invade Romania. The President wants to know if the Romanian Army and Civil Defense can hold the Soviet army off for twenty-four hours.

The President is making a decision whether to come to Romania's aid. He wants an answer in fifteen minutes. Get any and all the information you need. Here is the latest intelligence we have smuggled out of Romania. Translate what you can and give us an answer."

Jeed sat there dumbfounded. What in the hell was the President of the United States doing asking a lowly three-striped sergeant to make a decision that could mean World War III? Panic filled Jeed. This could mean nuclear holocaust! "Fifteen minutes," repeated the officer sternly. Jeed took the intelligence information, placed his headset back on, and immediately started reviewing it. He almost laughed. It contained the same stupid intelligence that all the previous material contained. But only he knew, because of his previous intelligence findings, that the Romanians had already called up the Civil Defense. The only added information with this new intelligence was that they had also mined every bridge between Bucharest and the northern borders. There was no way the Soviets could bring down the Romanian government in less than twenty-four hours. But was that really the point? Wasn't the President actually considering World War III? Extreme emotions paralyzed Jeed as he sat glued in his chair, pondering the fate of the world. What should he tell the President's people? What would it mean if he were wrong? Could the wrong interpretation bring devastating consequences to the world? Jeed's response would determine whether the world's mightiest armies would clash. Johnson was ready to drop paratroopers if need be. As the last of the fifteen minutes ticked by, Jeed began to laugh to himself. Should he laugh out loud? Surely they'd think he'd cracked. The whole scenario struck him as ludicrous. Who was running the world after all? The dramatic answer, he realized, was that no one was. No one could. World power was nothing but an illusion. Johnson was no greater than a three-striped sergeant at this moment in time. No man knew more about the possibilities of World War III than Jeed did at this moment in history. Nobody was really in charge. Nobody ever was. Did that mean that all this struggle between global powers was a joke? A fantasy? Jeed fully comprehended in that instant that the answer was yes. Just like what he had learned in winning the American Spirit of Honor Medal three years earlier, these were nothing but boys in men's bodies.

"Sir," Jeed announced, "the Romanians have mined all the bridges and have called up the Civil Defense. That means that every man who can walk has been enlisted. They are ready. The Russians probably are aware of this mobilization as well."

"Are you sure, Sergeant?"

"Sir, the Romanians knew three days ago that the Russians would not stop at Czechoslovakia. They can definitely hold the Russians for twenty-four hours." With that, the officer turned and marched out of the office with his flank of subordinates trailing behind. Weeks later, Jeed would find out that Tricky Dicky had called the Kremlin and had given the Russians an ultimatum, laying out in detail how the United States could stop the Soviet Army. No one knew that World War III had been placed on the table and that the Soviets had backed away. The Soviet High Command wanted no nuclear confrontation and no embarrassment. For centuries, Romania's geography had been the regret of many a conqueror. The reason why Romania's language to this day remains seventy-five percent Latin is a testimonial to its endurance. The Soviets were crazy to think that Romania would be easy pickings. The world was mad, and Jeed no longer wanted to be a part of it.

From that day forward, Jeed never again respected authority of any kind. No one, but no one, ruled over him after that. He became rebellious during his remaining days in the Air Force, refusing to produce any more intelligence reports other than to write "no reportable intelligence" across everything put on his desk. He was given an early out. Honorably. And just as well. He no longer believed in leaders or countries or political power or governments. All were illusions created by men who did not know their own personal boundaries, who could not respect the boundaries of others.

As Jeed gazed at Josh, he hoped that this newly accepted man would also understand the power of the human individual in harmony with the oneness of nature. So much of life is dictated to us. And it continues to be dictated because we surrender our uniqueness, our humanness, the magnificent power with which each of us is born. Each of us has the power to change the world in our own way, not unlike Jeed had in that fifteen-minute period one spring morning in 1968. Josh stood for a new kind of world. He and his kind, these Children of the New Earth, are like fertile seeds planted in the soils of an insane Earth, soon to change a world that could destroy itself.

Jeed reached into his pack and pulled out a book. He opened it to the bookmarked section and spoke. "Josh, it is time to talk about the fire that rests in a man's loins. I'm not going to talk about the birds and the bees. I'm going to talk about the bridge that connects the worlds of men and women. I'm going to read to you a section from a book called *Return of the Bird Tribes* by Ken Carey. This is the story of White Buffalo Calf Woman."

Jeed read how White Buffalo Calf Woman had come from the stars to grace the world of men. When she stepped upon a sea of rolling grasses, she met two warrior braves who were brothers. The first warrior brave, remarking on her extraordinary beauty, exclaimed how he would like to couple with her right there on the sun-warmed prairie. His brother responded by telling him to put away such thoughts, for this was a sacred woman not to be approached in such a manner. But surprisingly, the woman dressed in white buckskin invited the lusty warrior to come with her, for he would realize his desire. At a distance, the second brother watched as a cloud of dust surrounded the couple. After a while, White Buffalo Calf Woman stepped out of the dust cloud, retying her white buckskin dress. At her feet lay the corpse of the lusty brave, partially decomposed and crawling with worms, flies, and beetles. She said to the remaining brave, "A man who looks first to a woman's outer beauty will never know her beauty divine, for there is dust upon his eyes and he is as good as blind. But a man who sees in a woman the spirit of the Great One and who sees her beauty first in spirit and in truth, that man will know God in that woman; and should she choose to lie with him, he will share with her in enjoyment more fully than the former ever could. And all will be as it should" (*Return of the Bird Tribes*, Uni*Sun, 1988, p. 62).

Jeed continued to read the story of how this sacred woman taught the people many truths, telling the warrior brave how he and his brother symbolized two paths that men in a tribe could take. If a man first seeks the spiritual path, he will have eyes that see truly what the Creator sees. If a man first seeks the sacred vision of the Great Spirit, he will live a full life. But if a man seeks first earthly desires and forgets the spirit, he will die inside. She continued to warn the brave that most of the men of the day forget not only the Great Spirit, but forget what is divine within themselves. In turn, they contribute nothing to women and their womanhood and, in turn, nothing to their people. Jeed then went on to read how White Buffalo Calf Woman used fire from the brave's own campfire to light the first peace pipe. She presented the ways of peace to the brave, and then to his people. From the peace pipe hung twelve feathers, which were to remind the people of the feathered races, their spirit selves, the Bird Tribes, and the Winged Ones of Heaven.

"Josh," said Jeed, "do you understand what I am trying to say to you?" The lad's eyes left the fire and stared deeply into the eyes of his other-father. It was as if Josh had acquired the ability to see into Jeed's soul as Jeed had seen into his. Some ancient fire had ignited within Josh, and Jeed could see it starting to fill this initiated man.

"I think so, Jeed. I think so." Josh had nothing more to say, returning his eyes to the rainbowed flames.

"Then I am finished," pronounced Jeed, looking over at Chris.

In response, Chris lifted his sack in Santa Claus fashion and extracted a bundle. Carefully he unfolded his prize, a marvelous buckskin Jeed had given to him the year before up at Priest Lake. On the buckskin had been painted patterns by a local Native artist. An old shamanic pattern of striking geometric designs arranged in concentric circles had been painted in colors of black, red, and white in the midsection of the tanned skin. Lightning bolts passed through the center, giving the impression of a spirit gateway. As Chris fully unrolled the skin and held it up, his arms extended above his head.

"Josh, I would like to explain the meaning of the sacred patterns on this deer skin. One night, while staring at the designs, I saw the meaning. The meaning left me with a sense of never being alone. And I want you to know that you will never be alone." As he draped the skin over his right arm, Chris began to point to certain parts of the patterns. "You notice these circles of arrowheads and triangles that surround this circle in the middle? You are the circle in the middle, Josh. Around you are the different levels of spirits and angels who are here to help you. The farther out from the center of the circle you go, the greater the spirits who serve you. This is to let you know that you are constantly watched over. As a man, you may have times when you feel alone, called to make a decision that you alone may have to make. At times, you may even feel abandoned. But I want you to realize that no man is alone. You are never alone. We, as men, will try and help you as you continue through life, but when those who care about you are not available, there are other forces that are backups. It is my wish to bestow the knowledge, the feeling, the hope of such forces from other worlds, other dimensions upon you. I want to give you a blessing with this sacred design. I want to bless you as a man. So I would like to place this on you as I give my blessing."

Chris walked over to his son and awaited permission. At first, Josh didn't know what his father was waiting for. But then he realized that Dad was waiting for permission from a man, rather than instructing a boy. After Josh nodded his head yes, Chris laid the deer skin on his back. The top of the skin rested on his head as if it were a hood. The main design centered between his shoulder blades, the white and black geometric figures glowing in the darkening twilight. Chris placed one hand on Josh's right shoulder and the other over the design on his back, holding the skin in place. "Josh, as your father, I have tried to help you grow through your boyhood the best I could. I had a lot to learn myself. And, as every man does, I made a few mistakes. One of the greatest forces in a man's life is forgiveness. And one of the greatest things a man can learn is to forgive himself.

I have learned to do that. One of the things I ask of you is to also forgive me for any mistakes I have made in bringing you up as my son. In asking this of you, I hope to give you the knowledge and the power of forgiveness. Like me, you, too, will be in charge of your own journey through life now. I recognize that. I want you to know how much I love you as my son, how much I respect you for all you have endured today."

As the skin rested gently upon Josh, it began to shake slightly. The emotions he had sought to contain unleashed within him. Tears streamed down his face as he gently sobbed. Chris continued. "I ask all the circles of spirit beings, who come to the aid of humanity, to watch over you. May you ever know their guidance, their wisdom, and their love. May you learn to walk in love, see with wisdom, and speak with truth. My heart is always open to you, Josh. If ever you need me along your journey into manhood, I will be there for you."

The silent tears could not wash away enough of the pent-up emotions; he now wept openly, the sound of weeping echoing in the forest as well as in the hearts of those next to him. The weeping came not from regret or sorrow but from something powerful and loving. All were taken aback. The power of Josh's emotions suddenly moved into all. The beauty of the scene penetrated Jeed, filling him with awe as well as a sense of true completion. He bit his lip, trying to contain his own emotions as Josh unleashed his. Overwhelming love swept through Josh as he fully opened himself to his father's words, which carried with them an awesome power. Even Chris was caught off guard as he felt the depth of the sobs through his hand, felt the heaving of his son's chest through the deer skin as he released all the feelings built up throughout the long day. With the tenderness that only a loving father can give, Chris leaned over and held his son in his arms, his own head resting caringly on Josh. Chris had been right: Josh was the center, and all in his presence felt the power of his being. Fire, love, spirits, and men. These forces, this driving ancient power, poured into Josh. Such a power echoed across time, space, and consciousness. Chris now wept with his son. He wept for the boy, gone forever, and for the man now destined to change a world gone mad.

Jeed glanced over at Paul to keep himself from joining in the tears, the ache in his throat growing rapidly. Paul stared at the scene of his brother and father. His countenance bore the kind of smile that said this was just what he had hoped for his younger brother. He nodded small nods, approving the power of the moment, knowing that Josh would remember this moment for the rest of his life. *Hell, I'll remember this for the rest of my life,* he said to himself. He had never witnessed his younger brother showing such genuine feelings. Certainly, he had manufactured extremes in feelings when doing battle, when mimicking Bruce Lee during make-believe fights over make-believe issues. But this was not make-believe. This was as real as life gets. And Paul would cherish this moment for an eternity.

After a while, Josh calmed, wiping his nose on his coat sleeve. The fire was dying rapidly as the rain once again began to fall. Chris continued his blessing. "May life be good to you, Josh. May you live it to the fullest. If you ever need me, just say so, and I will be there."

"I know, Dad. Thanks." Josh, well known for his capacity for using many words, said nothing more. Nothing more needed saying. He pulled the deer skin around his shoulders as if it alone could protect him not only from the falling rain, but from anything that might befall him.

"I think Paul has something to give you," Chris finished.

Paul rose slowly from his sitting log, the light from the dying embers reflecting off his glasses. "Josh, I want you to know how cool I think you are. You are the best brother a brother could ever have. I feel honored to be able to welcome you as a man into my life. There is something I want to give you as a sign of our togetherness." From his pocket, Paul took out a pair of car keys. He held them up as they sparkled in the firelight. "Even though my car was given to me as a graduation present, I want you to know that I share it with you. I am giving you your own set of car keys. I only ask that you take care of the car when you use it, and let me know ahead of time when you need it so we don't cause each other any problems. I'm going to college and won't use the car during the day since I'll be taking the bus to the university. So you will be able to take the car to high school. However, you have to buy your own gas." Paul laughed. He knew buying gas would soon be a reality Josh needed to experience. Paul knew that learning to balance the desire to drive around with friends, and paying for it, would bring a test of values that would also bring new awareness to Josh's manhood. "I'm going to have you drive the car for the rest of the day, all the way back up to Seattle."

"Duuuude," said Josh, "I don't know if I have the energy to drive all the way. I'm exhausted."

"Well, you can drive as far as you're able. When you get tired, you have the power to ask for help. Either Dad or I can take over. But I want you to drive as far as you can, and I want you to understand the importance of asking for help when you need it from other men."

Josh accepted the keys and stared at them in his hands as if they were made of gold. A car. Freedom. Independence. So overwhelming. The whole day had been so overwhelming. He had never felt this way before and didn't quite know what these new feelings meant. But he had an idea. An idea somehow incapable of being spoken.

"Are we done?" asked Josh as he turned in Jeed's direction.

"Not quite. Let's have our closing ritual and then head out. We have a feast planned after this."

"Food? God, I could eat a horse!"

"Good" said Jeed. "But first we must close the ritual space by thanking the spirits and returning them to whence they came. It is a dishonor not to acknowledge the help we have been given. And it is unwise not to bid the spirit beings farewell. Strange things can happen when spirits are left to wander." He had learned this from Malidoma.

Malidoma had told of a ritual involving a group of men gathered at a conference where he had been invited to speak. The building sat on a Civil War site as a memorial, with a museum nearby. A terrible battle had been fought on this site, and many had died. Out of a sense of respect, several of the men at the conference had invited in the spirits of the dead soldiers during the opening ritual. But after the conference was over, no closing ritual had been planned. Malidoma had already left, not knowing of such folly. A few weeks later, the building had burned to the ground. From that point on, Malidoma made sure that attendees knew that whatever space they opened they were responsible for. When sacred space is opened, it must be closed in gratitude and respect.

Jeed turned in the four directions and gave thanks to all the spirit beings who had helped them that day. He then sprinkled water on the ritual fire, causing it to hiss and sputter as the steam rose into the rainy evening, swirling a farewell to the four men. The time had come for leaving.

"Chris, would you sing your closing song, your chant of thanksgiving?"

"Yeah, but let's circle around the fire as I sing it." He took the buckskin off Josh and carefully folded it, returning it to its bag. Joining the rest around the fire, brothers all, he sang loudly to the dying fire and to the falling rain, the song echoing through the forest. There were no more tears, only joy. The initiation was complete.

As they gathered up their things, Jeed announced, "OK, Josh, you get to pick any place you want to eat. What kind of place would you like to go to? Money's no object."

"Can we go to a restaurant like this? I'm a mess!" Jeed couldn't tell whether he was talking about his clothes or his hair. He hadn't seen so many hairs out of place on Josh's head since his junior-high days.

"Don't worry about it. If the restaurant doesn't like the way we look, they'll tell us, or they'll hide us in some corner. So what kind of food would you like?"

"Nothing too strong. My stomach is really complaining. How about Mexican food?" And off they went, Josh driving, with Jeed following behind in his jeep.

After the sumptuous meal, hugs were exchanged. Josh and Paul argued over who should drive back to Seattle. Paul insisted Josh drive until he got tired; Josh insisted he was already tired. But Paul countered that Josh should test himself with real driving. The whole trip back consisted of Josh complaining how tired he was. Paul would encourage him or suggest that they pull over for a while, or stop for coffee — or, in Josh's case, Jolt Cola, which he never drank but always talked about. The car pulled into the family driveway at ten at night — Josh still driving. Chris had remained strangely silent the entire trip, sitting in the back seat, watching his two sons banter back and forth about who should be driving. He saved his words for the end.

"I'd like to have a thanksgiving ceremony, a prayer, before we go inside. As a family, we have shared a lot today, been through a lot today. So I'd like to say this prayer of thanks for all that happened." Paul and Josh looked at one another with faces that said *Guess we'll have to humor the Old Man*. Chris switched on the overhead light and unfolded a piece of paper from his coat. In a clear voice he read an old Sioux peace prayer:

O, Great Spirit,
Whose voice I hear in the winds,
Whose breath gives life to the world,
Hear me.
I am small and weak.
I need your strength and wisdom.
May I walk in beauty,
Make my eyes behold the red and purple sunset,
Make my hands respect the things you have made
And my ears sharp to your voice.
Make me wise so that I may know
The things you have taught your children,
The lessons you have written
In every leaf and rock.
Make me strong.
Not superior to my brothers,
But to fight my greatest enemy — myself ...
Make me ready to come to you with straight eyes,
So that when life fades as the fading sunset,
My spirit may come to you without shame.
                    — Chief Yellow Lark, Lakota Sioux, 1887

Chris then folded up the paper, switched off the light, and led his two sons back to the house. Nothing more was said. The day had started in silence; only right to end it in silence. All would sleep like they had never slept before.

Chapter Twelve

SHADOWS

*T*he front door flew open as Josh and his friend Omar bustled through the living room with little more than a wave of the hand and a "Hi." Jane turned her head to catch Josh in midstride. "What's going on?" she asked.

Josh stopped long enough to acknowledge the question. "Omar is going to spend the night. We're going upstairs to check out my latest computer game."

"Uhhhh, nobody asked permission from me to see if Omar could spend the night."

"Mom!" Josh responded with isn't-this-obvious in his voice. "I don't need to ask permission. I am a man." With that, he bounded out of the living room and upstairs with Omar trailing closely behind.

Jane slowly turned her head to Jeed, her eyes wide with exasperation. "You did this," she said with a smile on her face.

Grinning back, Jeed said, "Well, I'll have to remind Josh about the part of the initiation where we discussed respect for others.

Saying you're a man does not make you a man. Perhaps a little reminder on how his actions have to match his words is in order. I'll wait till Omar leaves. I've been wanting to talk to Josh about another matter, anyhow."

Jeed had driven up from Portland to spend New Year's with the family. So much had happened since the initiation, so much had changed. And not just with Josh.

"It's amazing," said Jane, "how much different Josh is since he got back. We've talked in detail about rites of passage before the weekend of the initiation, but not much about girls. Do you think you could initiate girls into their womanhood the way you guys brought Josh into his manhood?"

"Y'know, that's a question that has been plaguing me. I'm not sure how to answer it. I know that many Native societies have rites of passage for the girls as well as the boys. However, it was the women who took charge of welcoming girls into their moon, as some call it. They make quite a ceremony about their period starting, and they create ritual to empower the girl into her womanhood. Could a man or men pull that off? I don't think so. Here's my slant on it. What I am really trying to do with these Children of the New Earth is more than a rite of passage into manhood or womanhood. I'm really trying to get them into a place of owning their powers, moving into a place of what I call 'Remembering.' This is all still sketchy for me. I really need to explore this more. But I believe what is key in getting them to this Remembering, this Awakening, is to get them to move into the Oneness. Malidoma's people had a different metaphor than what I'm looking at. They call this place where consciousness shifts the Otherworld. The path to the Otherworld is through Nature, with a capital en, which I am discovering is quite powerful and necessary. It includes the realm of the spirits associated with nature. However, I'm discovering that our modern society has different phenomena facing it. And these children, these gifted ones, are more about changing our present world than trying to fit into the world we are leaving them. Our world is a mess, and they know it. The ways of the indigenous societies and their rites of passage seem, to me, to be more about fitting into the ways of the tribe. Carl Jung put my point of view in an opposing perspective to that of the indigenous societies. He said that it is not the business of the individual to serve the community, but the business of the community to serve the individual. Much of indigenous initiation strikes me as being about moving their young ones into a place of belonging in the tribe. And I'm not sure that's what this phenomenon of the Children of the New Earth is about at all. I believe it's more the Jungian point of view. I believe we have let these kids down by not making it possible for them to change our world. I believe that such change has to come through Oneness. But how to get there?

"Frankly, I'm discovering that we must not expect them to fit into our ways. It's like visiting friends in France. Do you go to France and expect them to speak English? Or do you go there, learn French first, and then speak with them? Well, if you are the one who is hoping to impart something, hoping to engage or fully connect with your friends, it seems to me it would be much better to learn French. If I expect them to learn English, then I'm pretty much saying, 'You have to come up to my level.' If I'm the one who is trying to reach them, connect with them, I have to leave behind my arrogance. I need to meet them where they are, not where I want them to be. That being said, I believe women should initiate girls because I don't think a man can speak the language of womanhood to a girl. I mean, look at the way men, and even other women, talk about a woman's cycle. They use words like 'the curse' or 'on the rag' and usually in the most disrespectful way. There is no way they are recognizing the womanly essence of creation, cleansing , and rejuvenation. Nature has seen fit to keep men sexually away during this time of death and new life in the woman. But men typically see that they 'ain't getting any.' That the Mother, the Wife, the Woman, has been replaced by the Bitch.

"I can't sit here and say to girls, 'I know of the Oneness. I teach about the Oneness. If you want to learn from me, then you have to leave behind your dualistic ways. You have to find the path that leads to my ways.' So that says to me that I would be more effective working with boys and my fellow men in showing them the path I took to reach them. To show people the Oneness, I have to enter the biggest realm of dualism: the separation of the sexes. There have to be women out there who can lead girls into Oneness. Elders are equally necessary among women."

"Well, Jeed, you know how active I am with school programs. It seems to me that some kind of initiation is as needed for girls as it is for boys. Where would a parent go to find someone like you?"

Jeed thought about it a minute. "I don't know. There's a part of me that thinks a parent can't just go find an Elder like they would a head of lettuce at the grocery store. I'm not sure you could have found just anyone to work with Josh. And I suspect that would be true with others. Some part of me believes that these young people have to find their own Elders, and somehow, some way, the parent then has to bless it. I need to work with this more, explore the possibilities."

"And what about the work you do with angels and spirit beings? Certainly, not everyone believes in that. Could a girl be initiated by someone who doesn't believe in the spiritual?"

"I know there are people who do rites of passage who are not trying for the same thing I am trying to accomplish. Certainly, initiation could be done without the invitation of the spiritual forces. But then it wouldn't be ritual. It would be ceremony or it might be liturgy. Malidoma was quite outspoken about the differences. He felt ceremony was little more than a skit or an enactment. Even liturgy, which is performed in sacred space, has no power if the space is not shared with the Divine or with a spirit being. There are people who do rites of passage that are ceremonial, but that's all it is. Remember when Chris and I tried to initiate Paul? That was pretty much ceremony. And as a result, it had no power and no effect on Paul. From what I've heard in talking with Paul after Josh's initiation, Paul may have gotten as much or more out of the initiation than Josh did. And that was due to using ritual rather than ceremony. What I wanted for Josh was more than entry into manhood. I wanted him to fully embrace himself, his gifts, and his future. From what I can tell, a man or a woman cannot do that alone. 'It takes a village to raise a child.' And that 'village' extends into the sacred."

192

"All right. I can see that. But what if people aren't into what you're into? What if they don't believe in angels or power animals or plant spirits like you guys do?"

"Well, Malidoma certainly didn't believe as I do. In his case, the greater spiritual forces lay with what he called 'the ancestors.' Other cultures exist that believe in ancestral forces, even to the point of worship. The Egyptians often elevated their pharaohs to godhood, eventually to be worshiped. Some Native tribes had similar beliefs. There are many options available to different societies. Aborigines believe in the Dreamtime. Celtic tribes believed in animism. There also exists Wiccan spirituality. South American tribes believe in shamanism, animal cults, and nagualism, which Carlos Castaneda taught in his books about Don Juan. There are numerous options for these kids. Whatever works for them. Chris is really into Joseph Campbell. Campbell's work in mythology is unparalleled. But even he tells us we must come up with our own new myths. That is what I tried to do with Josh. With someone else, I might have done a different kind of initiation."

Jane wanted to know if others should know of what happened to Josh. A part of her thought others *should* know. But that meant she needed answers to questions that would inevitably come as to what other parents could do for their kids. "If someone were to ask you what elements would be needed to successfully initiate their son or daughter, what would you tell them?"

"Keep in mind that I am relatively new to this. I don't pretend to have all the answers. Keep in mind that when Chris asked me to consider initiating Josh, he wanted a better life for Josh, better than he ever had. That takes in more than a laundry list. So before I answer that question, I'd like to give an example of what I'm trying to say here.

"Before I came up here to spend New Year's with you guys, I saw this piece on TV on one of the news magazine programs. Might have been *60 Minutes*. The program had featured an interview with one of the most dangerous leaders of a gang in the L.A. area. Among gang-bangers, he was known as 'Monster' — a name he wore proudly."

Jeed went on to tell how the opening shot was of Monster behind bars. He was intelligent, he was handsome, he was ominous, he was arrogant, he was black. The interview was bone-chilling to listen to. This renegade of society was studying law while in prison. He had also written a book that was getting a lot of attention. The book's title was *Monster*. Watching him was like watching a scene from *The Exorcist*. He just kept sending shivers up Jeed's spine. If this guy represented gang leadership, then this country was in big trouble. What raw talent, what power, what righteous indignation he displayed. This gang leader played to the camera like an experienced Hollywood actor. He knew what he was doing, and he was doing it well. Jeed could only shake his head in disbelief. What misdirected power. What had made this guy such a monster?

The interview took a sudden turn as the reporter tried to parry with his subject: "Monster" Kody Scott. One glib tongue trying to outdo the other. There were questions of family, friends, neighborhood, and community. The reporter tried to tie up Monster with his questions as if he were trying to make a hangman's noose out of words. The story that came out of the answers shocked Jeed. Monster had everything going for him. He was a smart kid who had gotten good grades in the beginning. His father was a successful NFL football player. Famous. But had no time for his son, only his career. Failed marriage. The father rarely saw his son, leaving him to find another kind of family — on the streets, because Dad was never there. "I'll never forget this guy's answer to the most telling question from the reporter," said Jeed with the memory of it still in his mind. "Monster said, 'He wasn't there for me. I don't have any feelings for him. He doesn't have any for me.' And the camera zoomed in closer and closer. And there, on the edge of his eyelid, a tear started to form. When that tear slid down his cheek it was like watching Niagara Falls. All the violence, all the killing, the hatred, the coldness, the evil, betrayed by a single tear.

"There it was for the whole nation to see. A boy in a man's body, imprisoned by his own father's lack of love. And because he had been abandoned by his father, he now reaped vengeance on all of society, even from behind bars. Somehow, this monster meant to change what had happened to him. And he didn't care how he did it.

"That's what I think these Children of the New Earth are all about. I think they are here to change our world because our world needs changing. And if we don't let them change it through their giftedness, then they'll change it through their power, their ability to destroy and tear down. So I don't think I can give a list of to-dos that can be followed by just anyone."

"Nonetheless," said Jane, "I'd like to hear what you would do to initiate a girl if the opportunity presented itself."

Jeed had to think about that for a while. After entertaining some ideas and throwing out others, he decided that perhaps the following might work:

1. Help the girl find an Elder or Wise Woman in whom she can trust. Mothers should not initiate their daughters for the same reason why men should not initiate their sons. The mother is too invested in the girl to truly allow the woman to come forward. These Elders should have experience in the sacred or the spiritual, and they should be able to put that experience to use through ritual.

2. Include your spouse in the planning stages. If you are a single mother, strongly consider bringing in a male who knows and loves your daughter to help with the planning. In such cases, you may wish to have a series of rituals rather than a single major ritual, spanning a couple of years, to reduce the demands on time and responsibility involved with schedule coordination.

3. Don't copy ritual from other cultures except as a reference. There is a kind of fad in ripping off Native American rituals. If you aren't Native American, then don't insult those who are by coopting their sacred rites. It's important for us to come up with our own myths and our own rituals. Our Native

Americans have given us a rich legacy in what is called by some "earth spirituality." Learn from it, borrow from it, but don't copy it.

4. Give the Elder, the Father, and the Mother clearly defined roles. Don't have these roles divided or shared. It will only detract from the ritual and lessen it.

5. Bring other Wise Women into the ritual space. Encourage creativity and personal testimony. It will provide your daughter with a sense of community and archetypal support.

6. Acknowledge and instill Mystery. Mystery has always played an important role in the lives of humanity. So much of what happens in initiation is beyond explanation. Make that an essential part of the experience.

7. Do as much as possible in nature. This can't be overemphasized. Get as far away from the city as possible. There is a reason why gangs flourish in cities. Nature has a way of reminding us of our smallness and our interdependence on this planet. Weakness has been a key element in womanhood. For instance, rape virtually did not exist in Native American tribes that were based on matriarchal lineage. Woe be it unto any brave accused of raping a woman. For the women took it upon themselves to rectify the situation, usually with the brave being found dead and abandoned, later. Not being afraid of weakness is true strength. Women have given up too much power and allowed the strength of the patriarchal society to silence them. Those days must come to an end.

As Jane and Jeed were finishing their enlivening conversation, Chris entered the living room. He caught the tail end of the discussion and couldn't help but chime in. "This whole topic of initiation may be far more important than we realize, Jeed. In a strange way, I feel what happened in the Gorge may have affected me more than it affected Josh." He paused, waiting for any sort of reaction. Chris had a way of sniffing his nose whenever he was nervous or something was bothering him. Usually, this habit drove Jeed crazy, making him want to laugh because he couldn't help but think that it made Chris sound like he had the remnants of a cocaine habit. But this time he listened carefully. After the third sniff, Chris began again. "I keep waking up with these powerful dreams since the initiation. Jane says I've been screaming in my sleep. It's like a part of me is dying, an old part. I don't know what words to use except to say that I'm not sure this was Josh's initiation into manhood. Actually, I think it was mine."

Wow, Jeed thought. *This is taking an unexpected turn.*

"My father has been appearing to me in my dreams," Chris continued. "He doesn't appear to me as in real life. There is great joy on his face. In some instances he is reaching out to me. In other instances he asks me to forgive him. It's like he's come back from the grave. It's gotten me kind of rattled."

Malidoma had spoken often about the realm of the ancestors. In some sociological circles, dedication to ancestral spirits is termed the "cult" of the ancestors. Although Jeed had difficulty appreciating Malidoma's dedication to his ancestors, what he was hearing from Chris made him wonder whether he had dismissed Malidoma's opinions too quickly. Chris's story gave Jeed goose bumps as he wondered whether his own relationship with his father was trying to come into play. He, too, had been having powerful dreams. Dreams about being in jail. However, this was a jail that had an open gate. The problem was that none of the prisoners would leave unless someone led the way, someone took a chance. In the dream, Jeed kept trying to encourage the men to leave the jail, to free themselves. But they wouldn't leave. And Jeed would not lead the way. There they all stayed. Trapped in a jail with no locked gate. Jeed listened carefully to the rest of what Chris had to say.

"Jeed," Chris almost pleaded, "you've got to tell more people about these initiation rites. I'm beginning to think they are more important than either of us imagined. It's like my father has come back to make amends with me. What is even more amazing to me is that I've finally decided I can forgive him for abandoning us when me and my brothers were kids, for never being there for us when we needed him, for committing suicide in the end rather than clean up the messes he left in our lives. Something big in me has changed."

As Jeed listened, his heart began to pound wildly, his face grew hot. Why was this affecting him so strongly? He didn't know. There seemed to be a part of himself that he really didn't want to deal with. Some shadow had crawled over him, confusing him emotionally. "I'll give it some thought," he said. What had Chris tapped into? Did it have something to do with Jeed's own father? Was it possible to find some kind of ancestral healing by daring to submit oneself to a ritual that carried the consciousness of manhood far beyond that of just one single man? Was it naive of Jeed to assume that the initiation had only to do with Josh? As his face flushed even more, he realized he didn't want to know the answer. "I'd better have my talk with Josh while I still can. Who knows when he'll be out the door driving his friends around again?" And with that, he left.

"Josh, could we have some time to talk with one another?" The day had gone quickly with shopping trips and movies and plans for skiing the next day.

"Sure, Jeed. Where would you like to talk?"

"Anywhere in private is fine." And with that, Josh asked Omar if he could catch up with him later. After saying good-bye to Omar, Jeed sat on the floor with his hands clasped, feeling tension, not knowing where to begin. After reminding Josh of the part in the initiation where he was taught that a man respects others, Jeed revisited the scene downstairs with Jane. Indeed, others lived in the house, and it was only respectful to take their needs into consideration.

A smile came across Josh's face. "Dude, I was teasing her, pulling her chain. I thought she would figure that out. I'll be more careful next time."

Jeed nodded his head, understanding. Teasing was a big part of this family's dynamics. But what he had to say next hung in his throat. Slowly, he began. "Josh, I know how you hate secrets. Well, it's time for me to let you in on a secret I have been keeping from you for quite a while." Josh's face hardened. Already he didn't like what he was hearing. "When I accepted the role of Elder in your initiation, there were certain responsibilities I undertook. I discussed them with your mom and dad but decided not to with you. And I need to rectify that now. During the initiation, we spoke of how one's manhood is an ongoing journey. We either change or we die; and if we choose to die, we can die in more than one way. So many walk the planet dead inside because they refuse to embrace life as it visits them. As an Elder whom you have chosen, it is my role to be with you as you continue your journey, to assist you when you ask for it, to walk with you through your years along with the other men who have joined your circle. I have always told you that you are a gifted person. That was obvious to me and others even in your toddler years. During the initiation, I told you that I was an *adonisgi*, which in my tribe means I carry my own special gifts. My ancestors might have called me a medicine man or a shaman or even a translator, a walker between worlds. But there is another term that comes from the African tribes that might be even more appropriate. My friend Malidoma taught me about the gatekeepers. He told me that I was a gatekeeper. The word addresses the ability of certain men and women to work with other dimensions or other worlds. Gatekeepers are guardians of certain dimensional openings to alternate reality, called gateways. Now's not the time to talk about the life of the gatekeepers or all they are meant to do. I bring it up because it has to do with the secret I have kept from you. For the gatekeepers to move into or through these other dimensions, they cannot enter with a dualistic nature. That means they cannot bring attitudes or beliefs about good or bad, right or wrong, male or female through to the other worlds. The other worlds operate out of Oneness. And if a being moves into this Oneness carrying duality, then the forces of the other dimensions treat it as a contradiction, a chaotic force, and flush out any consciousness that holds on to the duality until it is resolved or balanced. In some cases, this contradiction of dualism entering Oneness can even result in loss of sanity or tremendous internal conflict or even death. With the help of Malidoma, I have discovered the meaning of what a gatekeeper is in modern society. I won't talk about gateways or gatekeeping right now. I'll save that for another day, another story, for there is quite a lot to tell. But for now I will deal with the problem at hand — the secret I've kept from you.

"In North America and South America, there exist Native traditions that have this gatekeeper in another form, called by various names like berdache, llahamana, winkte, or two-spirits. These terms connote sacredness, access to the Divine, ability to travel into other dimensions. In our American culture, this sacredness has been lost; it has been condemned and continues to be condemned. Nonetheless, before I accepted my mantle as your Elder, I should have informed you of what this means and who I truly am. I should have trusted you with the information so that you could have better understood all I was bringing from the Otherworld, so you could have better understood me and what I was trying to bring you. But I didn't.

"I feel bad for having not trusted you before now. I hope you will find forgiveness in your heart for that. Our society does not have a true translation for the gatekeepers or the two-spirits. The closest word we have is 'gay.' I am gay, Josh." Jeed searched the expression on Josh's face as he absorbed what had been told him. His head never moved, his breathing stayed steady, his eyes squinted. The silence between the two men continued for what seemed an eternity to Jeed.

Finally, Josh asked, "What about my dad?"

"Your dad? He's not gay. He's straight as an arrow."

"No. I mean does he know?"

Jeed laughed nervously at missing the obvious intent of the question. "Oh. Yeah. He's known for several years. Your mom knows too. I decided to tell Paul when he graduated from high school, before he started college."

"But you were married."

"It's called 'living in the closet,' and I was good at it for several years. Someday I will tell you the whole story about how I was 'outed' by an angel. But now, I have to ask if you still want me to serve as your Elder. Depending on your answer, I will also have to ask something of you."

Josh looked right into Jeed's eyes as if searching for his soul. "You are still Jeed to me. Nothing has changed. I love you like I loved Uncle Frank. I just don't understand why there have to be all these secrets."

"That's what I want to talk about. I hear what you're saying. But I feel I need to remind you of all the times I sat in this house and listened to your fag jokes and fag-bashing comments with your friends. I even made comments to you how it promoted bigoted thinking and bigoted attitudes in society as a whole. Uncle Frank, whom you greatly loved, was gay. And still you made comments. Do you know what that did to me and to the memory of Uncle Frank?"

Josh squirmed, ran his fingers through his hair, his eyes large with discomfort. "That's just stuff that guys at my school do. It's like making Polish jokes. And I'm part Polish. I don't do it much anymore. In fact, since the initiation, I don't do it at all. It's different for me now. I don't have to prove anything to anyone, I don't have to be part of the tough talk, the trash talk. Talking like that doesn't serve a purpose for me anymore. And, yes, I still want you in my life. I still want you to be with me as I grow, to be my Elder. Nothing has changed." The two sat silently for quite a while.

"OK" was all Jeed said. He knew not to make any more of the issue. They hugged for a long time, each feeling the other's wound.

As comforting as Josh's words had been, Jeed left Seattle still carrying a burden he could not identify. For the next year he wrestled with his burden. Was Chris right? Should he carry forward the story of the initiation? Should he try and help others? Or was there a part of himself he first had to address? A dark spirit that seemed to stalk him, a Shadow?

In an attempt to see and understand what others were trying to do with the topic of manhood, Jeed joined a Wisdom Circle near Portland, in the city of Vancouver, Washington. The Wisdom Circle, part of what was being called the Men's Movement, struck Jeed as a dead end after a while. Drumming began each meeting, which was nice. Drumming really gave one time to get in touch with stuck emotions or suppressed thoughts. But the dialogues afterward left no freedom for interaction. A talking sticks would be used. And only those who held the stick in their hand could speak. So there were no real discussions, or "cross-talk" as it was called, leaving little more than vapid interaction. The same talkers with the same issues tended to vent the same feelings meeting after meeting — variations on the same theme. And those familiar feelings grew boring week after week. To get around the rigidity, a group of men broke off to form their own private circle where friendships could honestly be built, and men could talk about anything they wanted. Jeed was invited to join the seven-man circle, and he accepted.

For the most part, the gatherings proved to be a resounding success as the men began to reveal more about themselves, sharing parts of their lives that they had hidden away or simply stifled — because that's what men did. Men kept feelings inside, hidden. As the group moved further into community, once a month sons were invited to attend. They ranged from toddlers to teenagers, and no matter what the age, they tended to look at the grown-ups with blank stares. Once the drumming was over they usually went outside to play, leaving the men to enter into heartfelt discussions. The sons enjoyed seeing their fathers do more than read the Sunday paper, but the gabfest did nothing for them. Oddly, it was the single men who challenged the fathers to come up with activities that would include the sons more. So outdoor events became part of the monthly get-together. A good time was had by all. But then it happened.

At one of the meetings, the fathers began to notice how they still weren't connecting with their sons the way they had hoped to. The notions of initiation and pre-initiation entered the discussion. All grew excited about the idea of how the boys needed to be readied for manhood. For the younger boys that would mean long-term preparation. For the teens, their age required that something immediate be planned. And that's how Beacon Rock once again invaded the world of men. A beginning ceremony was discussed. Jeed remained silent about the difference between ceremony and ritual. Each man would bring a symbol of himself to the opening ceremony to share with the boys. Whether that something was a song, or a game, or an object, the point was to bridge the chasm that had developed between fathers and their sons, between single men and married men. The date was set.

Jeed began to feel turmoil within himself as the day grew closer. Unlike others in the circle, he felt helpless to put into words the Shadow that still stalked him. He could not put a name to it, nor could he face it. Whatever "it" was. He carefully observed as the other men began to sabotage the event because of matters at work, or family problems. Others grumbled, resurrecting the word "commitment" to counter the delays. The date had been set, and everyone had agreed. "Be there or be square." Everyone had better show up. Men had to stand up for themselves, and more important, they had to stand up for their sons, setting a good example. The event had become a tug-of-war.

Two days before the scheduled hike up Beacon Rock, the weather changed. Heavy rains fell in the Gorge as they typically do in autumn. Certainly everyone knew that the date had been set. At the last minute, the fathers canceled out. Only two men showed up at the foot of Beacon Rock, Jeed and one other fellow who hadn't heard about the cancellation. Ironically, the weather cleared up, making for a rather nice hiking adventure. But only Jeed decided to make the climb. The more he ascended the craggy trail, the more turmoil began to boil within him. These fathers had wimped out on their own sons, and Jeed felt old wounds opening in him. Had not these fathers provided their sons with crossed signals once again? Rain was a de facto part of life in Oregon and Washington. All knew that. It's nothing to see shoppers in downtown Portland sporting nothing but a coat during a downpour. Rain was treated the same way in Portland that frost is treated in colder climes: you scrape it off and go on with your day. So what truly had stopped the men? As Jeed wound back and forth across the rock-face trail, he could come to only one conclusion. The fathers could do nothing for their sons because they themselves were still boys. *A curse on them*, Jeed thought angrily. *They have failed their sons.* Jeed's indignation grew stronger with each succeeding step. By the time he reached the top, he had to stop and let forth a bloodcurdling scream. He screamed again until tears flooded forth. Why was he so angry? What was possessing him? He could feel the Shadow take him as he screamed again and again. Like a spirit from the Underworld, the Shadow looked Jeed in the eyes, and Jeed beheld the face of his own father. The face of the man who had beaten his son so often to the point of bleeding. The man who had abandoned him, holding down two jobs because, as a husband, he couldn't stand to be in the same house with his alcoholic wife. The man who never had a kind word to say to his son. The man who had never shown his son love. Sobbing with grief that had built up through the decades, Jeed fell to the ground, hard. Realization tore into his heart, for he knew from his years of helping others that only one cure existed for him: he had to forgive his father. But he could not. His thoughts flew back to the moment that the God-Light had offered him forgiveness for having wasted so much of his life in the closet. He remembered how he could not forgive himself even in the presence of ultimate Forgiveness. This was the Shadow. And Jeed knew he could do nothing more for others until he first forgave himself, and then his father.

For seven years, Jeed went into hiding. For seven years he wrestled with his own torment. For seven years he wandered through the desert of his own woundedness. However, Josh blossomed during this time. He met his first girlfriend, fell in love, and broke up with her. He learned that love never dies but is only replaced by something better. His two closest friends got heavily involved in drugs, and wanted Josh to join them. He chose not to judge them, declined to walk their path with them, yet always remained available when they needed help. As much as it troubled Josh to be rejected for not joining his friends in their self-destructive behavior, he realized he had nothing to prove, nothing to gain by acting out their rage against a world that left them in pain and alone. Just as his father had prayed for him during the Ritual of Earth and Sky, Josh walked a firm path, a path he knew was his own.

The most difficult blow came when his best friend had to move away from Seattle after his sister had been raped by a gang member. Their family had pressed charges, only to be met with murder threats on the phone and in anonymous notes. Other gang members added to the threat at school. In the end, the rapist never even made it to trial, leaving the family little recourse but to flee the city in secret. Josh wasn't even told where his best friend had moved. No phone number, no address, nothing. Nothing seemed right about this episode. What the gang member had done reminded Josh of the warning of White Buffalo Calf Woman. But using flight to solve a problem also troubled him. Do we affect life, or are we affected by life? Josh had learned that we all have a choice. Surely, another way could have been found other than to disappear without a trace.

Josh also was voted by his peers to be a Peer Helper, an honor accorded to students who are seen as approachable, stable, and strong by fellow students. Peer Helpers are available night and day for those who might be facing suicide or bad drug trips or trouble at home. They help those who feel helpless, unable to trust an adult world that has not been there to show them the ways of wisdom, love, and inner strength. He wondered why others could not be initiated into the truth of their own power as he had been. Perhaps he would do something about that as he grew older.

Josh graduated from high school, having won one of the top scholarships in the state. When Jeed had presented him with the application form for the scholarship, Josh had said he didn't have a chance. Jeed then reminded him of similar words he had spoken on his trek up to the Pool of the Winds. As before, Josh broke through his self-proclaimed limits and submitted a computer design concept that won him a full-paid, four-year scholarship from the Washington Software Association.

The boy who had been afraid of anyone seeing his underwear now feared nothing. Who he was as a person, as a man, put him in a position of influence with others. All respected his tolerance, his ability to touch even the coldest heart, his desire to bring compassion into any situation. As he grew in years, so grew his gifts. His way was not the way of the many. Though he could have become a beacon of light shining before hundreds or even thousands, he chose to reach people one person at a time. For he knew that real change only comes one person at a time. Such are the beginnings of those who are here to change our world.

Jeed watched carefully as this initiated man continued his path toward fully becoming himself. After seven years of watching, Jeed finally confronted the source of his own Shadow. Only at his father's deathbed did he finally pronounce the words: "Dad, I want you to know that I forgive you for what you did to me and what you didn't do for me. I want you to know that I understand that you tried to do your best with me. I know you had a tough life. Your father abandoned you at thirteen. You had to quit school and provide for your sisters and mother by yourself. You were never very good at showing me love. I now realize that you, yourself, never really knew love. I forgive you for the way you hurt me — in my body, in my mind, and in my heart. I wish you peace that passes understanding." But Jeed's father could not hear him because he had already drifted into a coma, never to regain consciousness. But the powers of forgiveness are immense. They transcend death even more than they transcend life. Once again, Jeed could return to the way of the gatekeepers. Finally, he was whole. He now could forgive himself for his years of self-denial. He could enter fully into the depth of the Oneness.

BOOK TWO

WHEN STUDENTS BECOME MASTERS

Chapter Thirteen

WHEN THE STUDENT IS READY, THE MASTER WILL COME

*T*he *gods must be crazy*, Jeed thought as his yellow Geo Storm zoomed north on State Highway 17. Denver weather had baptized the trip with a torrential thunderstorm, nearly bringing traffic on Interstate 25 to a standstill. An hour later, Colorado Springs had followed up with a late-spring snowstorm that had cars skating across slush-laden lanes. Pueblo, not to be outdone, had finished the choreography with wind gusts that had sent the driver of the SUV in front of Jeed into a panic; he had hit the SUV's brakes with no warning, sending cars careening to either shoulder, barely avoiding a pileup. Jeed had driven just over a hundred miles, and had three close calls. *What in the hell is going on?* he asked himself.

Maybe he should never have started the trip. This was all Lorenzo's fault. The silver-tongued devil had talked Jeed into giving a keynote address as a favor to the conference organizer of the

Crestone Conference. She was a friend of Lorenzo's, and Lorenzo wanted both the experience and exposure that volunteering would bring him. This woman had a reputation for putting on small but profitable conferences, and Lorenzo had wanted to learn her secret. But unexpectedly losing the original keynote speaker with the conference date so close at hand had left her in a vulnerable position. She needed a name speaker to make up for the loss of her advertised Native American celebrity. Earlier, she had asked Lorenzo to help her with setting up the conference and making preparations. Volunteers made conferences more profitable. And Lorenzo had a big heart. Or maybe it wasn't his heart that was so big, but another part of his anatomy. He always had a hard time saying no to a pretty woman. Whatever the reason, Jeed had not only grudgingly agreed, he had also invited Renzo, as he liked to call his buddy, to co-present his workshop on "Radical Healing Techniques." Jeed had taught Renzo many of the techniques and had used his close friend in previous workshops, based upon the books he had written over the last several years. And Renzo loved a crowd — Jeed didn't. The author's books had pulled him unwillingly into the public limelight, kicking and screaming the whole way. However, the truth be told, he'd also become a first-rate lecturer over the last three years, as well as an intriguing interview on many alternative talk-radio shows. It wasn't that Jeed found giving a keynote address to be difficult; he just didn't enjoy it. But that Renzo — him and his silver tongue — he could sell doorknobs at a teepee. Yep, this was all his fault.

As Jeed aimed his yellow bullet north through the town of Alamosa and into the San Luis Valley, he began to fume all over again, replaying the scene that had almost caused him to cancel the Crestone engagement. Jeed had learned the ins and outs of being a keynote speaker over the years. There were courtesies he had become accustomed to. And the conference presenter had not gotten back to him about his room reservations or speaking schedule or food arrangements or whiteboards or tables or complimentary vendor space. In passing, Jeed had mentioned to Renzo that little communication had occurred from the presenter. It was then that

Renzo let his friend know that she had made all arrangements via Renzo. "And why you?" Jeed wanted to know.

"Well, because I'm helping her out with most of the conference arrangements, and I think she thought I'd take care of giving you the information since we're in the same house."

"And why haven't you?"

"What do you mean? What are you needing?" Jeed went through the list.

"Well, we're sharing a room. There aren't a lot of rooms at the lodge."

"What do you mean we're sharing a room? Why wasn't I asked?"

Renzo paused for a second, sensing he was in trouble. Choosing his words carefully, he answered, "I think it's because we're good friends. She just assumed we could share a room together."

Jeed's eyes narrowed. "I don't know if you noticed or not but I'm gay. Have you taken that into consideration? If I can avoid it, I don't share rooms with straight men. It's too much of a distraction. And this is business."

"What do you mean?" Renzo couldn't believe his ears. "You've been staying in my house for two months now. Are you trying to tell me that it's inappropriate?"

"No. Your room is on the top floor and mine is in the basement." Even then, Jeed could hear everything Renzo did in his bed through the ventilation ducts. The basement had not been insulated, and Jeed had excellent hearing. "Renzo, when I'm on the road, I like having a room to myself. Why didn't the conference organizer ask me if I wanted a roommate? She knows as well as you that I'm gay. Would she have assumed it was OK for a female speaker to room with you without asking her?"

"Probably not."

"Then you can see my irritation for not being asked about rooming with you?"

Renzo wore a smile on his face that resembled that of a man who'd just eaten smartenin' pills, and afterward was told that they were, in truth, rabbit turds — the classic punch line being "Now you're gettin' smarter." A blush rose in his face as he realized that Jeed wasn't kidding. The two often had mock arguments, not unlike two of the Three Stooges. Since Jeed's being gay hadn't bothered Renzo in the slightest, it had never occurred to him that his being straight would be a problem. Never in his life had being straight been a problem. For the first time he could recall, he felt separated by his own sexual preference. *Weird*, he thought. *Is this what discrimination feels like?* "So what do you want me to do? Do you want me to call the organizer and see if I can get you your own room? I don't think there are any rooms left. She was having a problem fitting all the speakers in. But if you want me to, I'll call her and try to explain."

"That would be nice," Jeed concluded. "Renzo, business is business. I don't like mixing personal matters with business matters. That's just the way I operate. It's part of what makes me good at what I do."

The disagreement had not stopped there. Renzo had been right. No more rooms were available. So Renzo had agreed to sleep in a tent down the road at a campground. Jeed felt embarrassed, and then angry about the whole affair. He agreed to stay just one night, give his keynote in the morning, and then leave. Renzo could then have the room to himself. Jeed wouldn't have any time to visit the exhibits or talk to the other speakers, but that was fine with him. He just wanted the whole to-do over with. But leave it to Renzo. Not a week had passed before Jeed found out that Renzo had decided to invite his girlfriend Carla to stay at the conference with him. Jeed started another round of confrontation with Renzo.

"Didn't you even hear me last week? I said I don't like to mix business with pleasure. You are my co-presenter. I don't want distractions. We're going to need to go over our talk. I'm going to need you to set things up, coordinate the book sales, and make sure everything is ready. When are you going to have time to take care of a girlfriend? Plus, the organizer has you doing everything but making her bed for her. This whole thing is looking worse and worse."

Renzo folded his arms. He'd had enough hassles from the conference organizer over the room situation. And now this. "You know what you need?" he said, sucking air between his teeth with his tongue. "You need to get laid."

"Funny, Renzo. It's obvious that's what you plan to do. I'm giving you an opportunity to speak before a conference. And I'm doing it because you deserve it. That kiss-ass organizer would sooner eat cactus than let you speak before a crowd. You're nothing more than her boy right now, taking care of everything she should have taken care of weeks ago. Don't give me shit. I'm trying to help you out here. And I'd like the same in return, if you don't mind." The glue that had held their friendship together was their ability to always say whatever they felt to one another. Jeed's favorite line to Renzo was "I didn't get to be this old for nothing. You're looking at fifty-five years of survival." They trusted who they were with one another. No secrets. Renzo's forty years, including his years in business managing customers and bank loan applications, made him a master in a crowd of people. His friendship had proven of great value to Jeed, who'd rather be by himself writing. Normally, Jeed treated folks with kid gloves. But when it came to business, he acted more billy goat than kid. Renzo had been caught by surprise.

"Jeed, I've already told Carla she could come. She plans to help out. You want me to call her up and tell her I've changed my mind because you have a burr under your saddle? Take it easy. It'll all work out. You'll see."

Jeed grumbled with exasperation. Why couldn't Renzo see how complicated he was making everything. Or maybe it wasn't Renzo. Certainly Jeed had heard before how he had gotten worked up over nothing. He wasn't called "the drama queen" by his friends for nothing. Maybe Renzo was right. "All right," he finally said. "But let this be a lesson to you. If you want to continue doing workshops with me, you've got to be focused and quit trying to make everybody happy. In the end, nobody is happy."

"Jeed, you really do need to get laid." Renzo let out a laugh, diving at Jeed with a flying leap, hog-tackling his best friend, tickling him unmercifully. Jeed squirmed defenselessly, screaming for mercy. Since childhood he could do nothing in a tickle fight. Nature had cursed him with this great weakness. And Renzo knew it.

The sagebrush and yucca plants zipped by as Jeed approached the turnoff to Crestone. The Sangre de Cristo Mountains to the east and the San Juans to the west flanked the arid valley floor with a contrasting beauty that hinted why this area had been identified as sacred by local Native Americans long ago, and now by New Consciousness enthusiasts. In the distance, the Great Sand Dunes Monument loomed like a misplaced mirage against the richness of the mountains. Had strange aliens kidnapped part of Saudi Arabia long ago and inadvertently dumped it in the middle of the Colorado mountains? A shiver rippled along Jeed's backbone. *What a strange yet inspiring place*, he thought.

Even the road before him stretched forth like a mystery. *Who would hold a conference in such an isolated place?* Few cars passed by from the opposite direction. The shoulder hugged the highway closely with about a foot of sand and loose gravel before desert scrub took over. If there were any car trouble, one would have to find a bare spot to pull off for repairs. During rainy spells, like he had just escaped on the other side of the mountains, the valley floor took on a flush of green, but during arid times like this, dead brush, and graveled sand left one with the impression that legions of wraiths had sucked the life out of the area, leaving behind the desert.

With the speed limit posted at sixty-five, Jeed pushed his hatchback to seventy. He hated being late for anything. And Renzo, along with the conference organizer, had scheduled a dinner meeting around five. But where was the turnoff? Surely he should have seen it by now. He decided to pull out the map and take a quick peek to see how close he was to Moffat, the next town up. The mileposts along the road would let him know. As he placed his finger on the map, his eye caught a glimpse of a road sign with the name of the road coming up. And as he took his eye off the road, the front right wheel of the Storm drifted onto the soft shoulder. Before he knew it, the car lurched to the right, catching more of the shoulder. Panicking, Jeed cranked the steering wheel left, swerving the back end of the Storm into the loose alluvium. A cloud of dust erupted as Jeed tried to lurch the front end back onto the highway. His oversteering jerked the whole car into a spin, propelling it across to the opposite lane. As much as he tried, he could not pull out of the spin. He might as well have been driving on ice. A combination of thrill and dread swept through him as he smacked backward against the soft shoulder of the left lane, catching one side of the car as the other lifted off the highway. As if in a slow-motion dream, he stopped breathing as the car began to somersault in midair. While upside down, the car hit the ravine fifteen feet past the shoulder. Glass shattered everywhere. As the car continued its somersaulting, a heavy object bashed the right side of Jeed's head. Silence. Darkness. Dirt and dust filled the interior of the cab. When would it end? The car flipped over one more time, landing upside down. Jeed sat motionless, his hands resting on the ceiling, now covered in dirt. Sound returned to his ears. *Am I going to die?* he asked himself. It struck him soberly that the car had been mangled and that the gas tank might explode any second. He had to get out. *Out! Out!* echoed in his head. He'd lost his glasses but he could tell the driver's side window had blown out. He had to get out. Immediately he reached for the safety belt. His hand tried to free the buckle. It wouldn't give. His weight from hanging upside down, along with the dirt in the buckle's catch had frozen the latch. He was trapped. Maybe someone would rescue him. His ears pricked up. Nothing but desert silence. His cell phone. He might be able to call 911. Where was his cell phone? His hands fumbled across the sand and grime. Water was everywhere. Water? The half-gallon water jug must have shattered. Everything seemed to be turning gray. Darker and darker. He was losing consciousness. He knew it. Was he going to die?

... to be continued

215

The trilogy continues ...

Book Two: INDIGO RISING: When Students Become Masters
estimated publishing date ... 2006

Book Three: INDIGO RISING: Meta-Parents for Meta-Children
estimated publishing date ... 2007

About the Author

G.W. Hardin is the author of *The Days of Wonder* and co-author of two other books: *The Messengers*, which hit bestselling lists all over the country for three months, and *On the Wings of Heaven*, a true story of angelic messages for humanity. The author's commitment to bringing controversial and important messages into public awareness, along with his unique blend of compassion and tolerance, has been put to the test and proven solid, as evidenced by the thousands of heartfelt letters sent by listeners and readers from around the world.

GW Hardin

At ease with diverse crowds, the Hardin is able to hold his own whether appearing as a lecturer or before an interviewer. His ability to handle talk-radio call-in guests who range from spiritual seekers to fundamentalists to confused questioners has been demonstrated repeatedly. Talk-show hosts such as Paul Gonzales repeatedly describe Hardin's airtime as "the best show I've done this year." TV host, Georgia Shakti-Hill (Wisdom Channel) echoes that sentiment.

A graduate in mathematics at the University of Washington, starting his career as a computer scientist, Hardin's encounters with angelic messengers convinced him to turn his attention to writing and bringing these stories forward

OTHER BOOKS BY GW HARDIN

THE MESSENGERS: A TRUE STORY OF ANGELIC PRESENCE AND A RETURN TO THE AGE OF MIRACLES
    by Julia Ingram & GW Hardin

This extraordinary book recounts in spellbinding detail the experiences of a prominent businessman who, initially skeptical, discovers under hypnosis an incredible past life as Paul the Apostle, one of the most powerful and influential disciples of Jesus.

OUT OF PRINT ... available at Amazon.com — used books

THE DAYS OF WONDER: DAWN OF A GREAT TOMORROW by GW Hardin

"A beautiful teaching book, a guide to mankind's new educational and spiritual aspirations: information instead of indoctrination, enlightenment as a result of the new education. Written with love and told with great consideration and compassion for the all but solutionless problems of the peoples of the world."
    — Maria Elena, renowned artist & author of Maria Elena's Mexico

Paperback, $14 plus shipping. Ask for book by name. Credit card recommended. Call toll free: **888-281-5170**

ON THE WINGS OF HEAVEN: A TRUE STORY FROM A MESSENGER OF LOVE by GW Hardin and Joseph Crane

Who would believe this story is true? Take a journey where Heaven and Earth meet in the unexpected friendship between a man and an angel.

Paperback, $17.95 plus shipping.
Order at gwhardin.com or Amazon.com

ON THE WINGS OF HEAVEN: A TRUE STORY FROM A MESSENGER OF LOVE by GW Hardin and Joseph Crane

Audio CD in MP3 format
Adobe Reader format. $14 plus
    shipping.
Order at gwhardin.com

THE MESSENGERS: A TRUE STORY OF ANGELIC PRESENCE AND A RETURN TO THE AGE OF MIRACLES

by Julia Ingram & GW Hardin

Audio tape
Order on Amazon.com or
www.gwhardin.com

9 781893 641075